A TIME TO DANCE

The Mike Cullen Story

as told to

DON RANLY

"We will not allow the state to decide who our brothers are."

— MICHAEL DENIS CULLEN

The Messenger Press
Carthagena Station
Celina, Ohio 45822

Prologue by Bishop Charles Buswell

Cover Design by Joan Giehl

PROLOGUE

By Bishop Charles Buswell

Bishop of the Diocese of Pueblo, Colorado

The war in Southeast Asia has dominated the American scene throughout our entire generation. It dramatizes the violence of which we as a nation are capable. The unspeakable holocaust at Hiroshima remains with all its guilt upon the American conscience. Far from admitting our guilt and from showing any willingness to repent we continue our violence in maddening and all too horrible proportions.

The killing has gone on for years. As of this moment more than one million military dead have been counted according to United States Government statistics released in late April, 1972. God alone knows the number of civilians who have met a violent death, thanks to the remarkable progress of American technology as developed to such perfection by Honeywell of Minneapolis and other United States' corporations.

To save face we go on killing! United States' bombers are continuing their work of devastation. No matter what the President had promised three years before, no matter how many United States' troops have been withdrawn, the war is as bloody as ever.

Ostensibly we have to be 'loyal' to our allies in South Vietnam. What does this 'loyalty' mean? The South Vietnamese just want the war to end! They are tired of being 'liberated' — liberated

5

from their homes, from their country and so very often even from their very lives.

There is a ballad which is entitled, "Where Have All The Flowers Gone?" This ballad repeats over and over again the refrain, "When will we ever learn?", "When will we ever learn?".

During the course of the past ten years or more contemporary prophets have been trying to teach us. We have heard the voices of the priest-brothers Berrigan. We have heard the voice of Martin Luther King. The voice of Rabbi Abraham Heschel still makes itself heard. Their prophetic utterances tell us of the evil of war and of all violence and call our nation back to decency, to humaneness and to the sacredness of human life — yellow as well as white.

One such eloquent prophetic voice is that of Michael D. Cullen, a man most gentle, a man saturated with the spirit of Jesus, a man whose handbook is the Bible, the Word of God. One of the adjectives which Michael Cullen uses often is a word which can aptly be used to describe him. He is an "incredible" man.

The actions of Michael Cullen have been performed with rare courage. He has been willing to speak out in prophetic fashion against the war, against violence, against American racism. He has been willing to sacrifice his own freedom and with even greater generosity he has jeopardized the future not only of himself but of his wife and of his children. He has left himself vulnerable to the possibility of deportation from this country that he loves in order that he might be a prophetic witness to his belief in the integrity of humanity, to call back all Americans to a sense of moral integrity, to accentuate the beauty of life and to recall to our minds that peace won at a great price can be preserved and promoted at an even greater cost.

Michael Cullen's spirit is that of the early leaders of the Christian community, who having been brought before the political leaders of their nation in their own day for teaching what Jesus taught and for living out this teaching could answer simply their accusers, "We must obey God rather than men."

This is Michael Cullen's message.

He speaks it with characteristic eloquence in Father Don Ranly's, "A Time to Dance." His words are words which all Americans should read prayerfully and reflectively . . . and now.

Prologue

By Don Ranly

A parish bulletin of Child Jesus church in Dublin, Ireland carried the following story in the spring of 1969:

"One of the most spectacular series of events on the American protest scene over the past year has been the trials of groups of young men and women who have burnt army draft cards as a gesture against the Vietnamese War. Often these trials have been showy and the defendants sullen and extremist. Recently one of these cases in Milwaukee got a lot of publicity in the American Mass Media. The group of protesters in question were known as the 'Milwaukee 14.' The last to be tried made a big impression by his quiet Christian attitude in court. He was a young man named Michael Cullen — an Irishman and an ex-butcher from Bray, Co. Wicklow.

"Michael Cullen gave a long testimony in Court which impressed everyone present. He didn't attack the war so much as plead that his conscience dictated that he make his draft card protest. He believed as a Christian that he had to draw attention to the militaristic and materialistic American scene. He quoted the Gospels and spoke of the message of peace of Jesus Christ. He said that his Catholic upbringing in Ireland had taught him the value of spiritual realities and that this was what modern America needed. According to reports of the trial in the newspapers even the judge felt that what Cullen said was strangely true.

"Cullen had earlier given up a good job and with his wife had opened a centre for the poor dregs of humanity of the large city of Milwaukee.

7

"Mike Cullen is someone we can be proud of on the swinging U.S. protest scene."

The action of the Milwaukee 14 — the napalming of Selective Service draft files — occurred on September 24, 1968. In January, 1970, I was with Mike for nearly twenty-four hours without interruption. We started talking in the early evening and at 3:00 a.m. I insisted that we get a few hours of sleep.

The next morning we turned the tape recorder back on and talked until 6:00 p.m.

Of course, I had known Mike and Netty and their three children long before this, mostly through their work for the poor at Casa Maria. But it was after this interview that I knew for certain that the life story of this twenty-eight year old man who had lived several full lives had to be written.

Just when was a problem. Undeniably, timeliness was important in terms of the message which needed to be told. Yet, so much of Mike still had to happen — the trial (the interview, Mike often says, was the dress rehearsal for his five-hour testimony at the trial), the sentencing, his jail experiences.

The real truth is, of course, that the Mike Cullen story will always be timely. It is a story for all times and all places. It is the classic story of the conflict of man versus the state, of private conscience versus the common law. It is the story of Joan of Arc, Thomas â Becket, Thomas More, Franz Jagerstatter, etc. etc.

Details may change. Wars may come and go, draft laws (involuntary slavery) may change. States, however, will continue to claim the right to determine who may live and who must die, judges will sentence men to dungeons for the sake of justice, racism will shift colors and nationalities, men and nations will continue to play god.

But history has always turned up men who say no. Long after they are dead other men will call them heroes, will canonize them, will term them prophets, martyrs, and will recognize their contribution to history. And at some other time in history, another man may be somehow inspired by their example to look into the depths of his own soul, and in utterly desolate loneliness, for reasons he himself does not understand, be compelled to say no, to follow his conscience; no matter the cost or the odds or the size and strength of the majority opposing him.

Mike Cullen (and the rest of the 14) does not make himself out to be a hero. He doesn't know, nor does anyone else, what the future holds for him. Perhaps he will "just" be a husband, a father, a laborer, a common man the rest of his days.

But no one can deny that Mike Cullen once said no to the system: first, by dropping out of the materialistic rat race and instead, feeding,

8

clothing, and housing the poor; second, by shouting a loud no, heard round the world, to the most ghastly, the most powerful, the most awesome death machine in the history of the world.

This book tries to say why. It talks about the people and places and experiences in his life which made him, a successful businessman, father of three, do the irrational, the impractical, the madly absurd act which he truly expected to cost him everything.

This is Mike's book. No one could possibly imitate his uniquely alive and poetic expressions. From talks with him years ago; from our extended taped interview; from other countless hours of visits and interviews at Casa Maria, in the Sandstone prison, and on the farm in northern Wisconsin where he lived for a time after prison; from visiting and living with his mother and father and family in Ireland; from talking to his monk and lay teachers and his spiritual director at the monastery in Roscrea, Ireland; from witnessing the whole trial, and especially from his testimony which spellbound a courtroom for five hours, I have arranged and re-arranged, selected and edited what appears here — all with Mike's final approval. The trial testimony was used wherever possible and I have indicated its use in the text by placing it in parentheses. My chief task in all of this was to transfer a charismatic oral communication to a somewhat accepted literary style in the printed medium, while preserving the real Mike Cullen. Anyone who knows Michael, knows that this is a difficult task. For Mike speaks in poetry, with a flair and a bounce, with a sparkle in his eyes and a lilt and a laugh in his voice, with style and imagination and a great, great deal of humor and humility, not taking himself too seriously but recognizing the Church and the times as bigger than himself.

In the many months that I have absorbed Michael, people often asked me why I was writing the book. Sometimes my answer was brief and simple. I would tell them that the Mike Cullen story had to be told for the same reason that people climb mountains — because they are there to climb.

I was convinced, always, that even if the manuscript were never published and even if no one ever read what was written, it had to be written.

But more practically, this story had to be told because less than ten years ago, Mike Cullen came to the United States still believing the words on the Statue of Liberty; still believing that America was the last hospitality house in the world, that here the poorest of the poor, the tired, the hungry, could come to make a decent living; still believing that in the United States, freedom and justice for all, regardless of race, creed, or color, was more than a slogan.

What happened to this country in those ten years?

Mike came to this country as a Catholic missionary, to be a priest in the solid and centuries-old tradition of Roman Catholicism in Ireland.

What happened to the Catholic Church in those ten years that made him, in large part, question that formal institution?

Just as Mike Cullen was compelled to look more closely at his adopted land, so he was driven to look more deeply into his faith. When he did so he felt the urge to return to the primitive teachings and to the life-style of the early Christians of the Gospels. Yesterday's generation, today's generation and tomorrow's generation will have to face one totally certain fact: the life of Mike Cullen, including his action with the Milwaukee 14, has been built on and inspired by faith — the Christian faith as it has come to us through the centuries. Mike Cullen is a man who read the Gospels, understood them, believed them, and acted in accord with them. No one could be raised more strictly or more traditionally a Roman Catholic. Michael has done what he has done, not in spite of his Catholic Christianity, but precisely because of it.

Hence, the book is a tribute to faith in our times, when so many would like to discard all religious truth and values. The book is a song of life, of joy and dancing in the face of death, when so many, without faith, are filled with hopelessness and despair. It is a book of radical Christianity, of radical Catholicism in the best tradition of Dorothy Day and the Catholic Worker Movement, of a simple living-out of the beatitudes, of total non-violent pacifism.

Nevertheless, if I am honest, I prepared this book because the words contained here express better than I could have myself, my deepest concerns and beliefs.

For this, I personally, will be forever indebted to Michael Denis Cullen and to his wife and to all the men and women of history who made him what he is.

THE STATEMENT OF THE MILWAUKEE 14

(September 24, 1968)

Generation after generation religious values have summoned men to undertake the words of mercy and peace. In times of crisis these values have further required men to cry out in protest against institutions and systems destructive of man and his immense potential.

We declare today that we are one with that history of mercy and protest. In destroying with napalm part of our nation's bureaucratic machinery of conscription we declare that the service of life no longer provides any options other than positive, concrete action against what can only be called the American way of death: a way of death which gives property a greater value than life, a way of death sustained not by invitation and hope but by coercion and fear.

We confess we were not easily awakened to the need for such action as we carry out today. In order for communities of resistance to come into being, millions had to die at America's hands, while in the process millions of America's sons were torn from family, friends, health, sanity and often life itself. Victim and executioner have been trapped in the same dragnet of death.

We have had to trace the roots of the Vietnamese struggle and suffering and admit that all too many of those roots converge in the soil of American values and priorities.

And we have had to adjust to the discovery that in that same soil have been engendered many of the other tragedies already underway. At home and abroad, opponents of America's economic, political and military commitments share with the innocent death by overt violence and the gunless violence of the status quo: death by starvation and mal-

11

nutrition, death from despair, death from overwork and exhaustion and disease. America, in the meantime, celebrates its "way of life": the canonization of competition and self interest, a high standard of living which rests on the backs of the poor. The values of brotherhood, joy, liberation and love become less and less comprehensible to our society. The world's wealthiest, most heavily-armed people, inheritors of a nation born in genocide against the Indians and built in great measure upon the toil of slaves, suffocate beneath myths of freedom and popular political control. Leaders of the religious establishment — preoccupied with mortgage payments, film-ratings, pills — automatically conscript the Creator of life into the ranks of America's high command, leaving others to apply the prophetic message they ritually recite. Vietnamese burn, Biafrans starve, tanks dominate the streets of Prague: at home Americans buy diet colas and flesh (that is, caucasian) colored bandaids, see dissenters clubbed to to the streets, counsel the poor to patience, cry out for law and order. . .

The tragedy worsens. While the number of American casualties in Vietnam has doubled during the past year, and the number of bombing raids nearly tripled since the President's "de-escalation" announcement of March 31, the very fact of U.S. discussions with the North Vietnamese has convinced many previously dissident Americans that their government now desires a peaceful settlement. The presence of American soldiers in anti-revolutionary struggles elsewhere in the world goes unobserved.

For a growing number of us, the problem is no longer that of grasping what is happening. We know it by heart. Ours is rather a problem of courage. We wish to offer our lives and future to blockade, absorb and transform the violence and madness which our society has come to personify.

We who burn these records of our society's war machine are participants in a movement of resistance to slavery, a struggle that remains as unresolved in America as in most of the world. Man remains an object to be rewarded insofar as he is obedient and useful, to be punished when he dares declare his liberation.

Our action concentrates on the Selective Service System because its relation to murder is immediate. Men are drafted — or "volunteer" for fear of being drafted — as killers for the state. Their victims litter the planet. In Vietnam alone, where nearly 30,000 Americans have died, no one can count the Vietnamese dead, crippled, the mentally maimed.

Today we destroy Selective Service System files because men need to be reminded that property is not sacred. Property belongs to the human scene only if man does. If anything tangible is sacred, it is the gift of life and flesh, flesh which is daily burned, made homeless, butchered — without tears or clamour from most Americans — in Vietnam, Thailand, Cambodia, Laos, Peru, Guatemala, Bolivia, Colombia, Nigeria, South

12

Africa, Harlem, Delano, Watts, and wherever the poor live and die, forgotten people, the anonymous majority. So property is repeatedly made the enemy of life: gas ovens in Germany, concentration camps in Russia, occupation tanks in Czechoslovakia, pieces of paper in draft offices, slum holdings, factories of death machines, germs and nerve gas. Indeed our nation has seen, with such isolated exceptions as the Boston Tea Party, devotion to property take ever greater precedence over devotion to life. So we today, in the face of such a history, proclaim that property has sanction only insofar as it serves man's need and the common good.

We strike at the Selective Service System because the draft, and the vocational channelling connected with it, are the clearest examples at hand of America's marriage to coercive political methods, exercised within as without its borders. In destroying these links in the military chain of command, we forge anew the good sense of the Second Vatican Council: "Man's dignity demands that he act according to a free conscience that is personally motivated from within, not under mere external pressure or blind internal impulse." (Constitution on the Church in the Modern World.)

We use napalm because it has come to symbolize the American way of death: a merciless substance insensitive to life and the sound of the human heart, blind to human pain, ignorant of guilt and innocence. Indeed napalm is the inevitable fruit of our national un-conscience, the sign of our numbness to life.

Finally, we use napalm and strike at the draft as a point of continuity in the non-violent struggle recently carried forward in Maryland. There, last November four resisters, using their own blood, stained the Baltimore draft records. And again, last May, a community of nine burned the 1-A files in Catonsville. At that time they declared, as we declare today, "Some property has no right to exist."

We have no illusions regarding the consequences of our action. To make visible another community of resistance and to better explain our action, we have chosen to act publicly and to accept the consequences. But we pay the price, if not gladly, at least with a profound hope. Just as our own hearts have spoken to us, just as we — not long ago strangers to one another — have been welded into community and delivered into resistance, so do we see the same spirit of hope and courage, the same freedom pouring into others: joy surprisingly is made possible only in the laying aside of plans for a comfortable, private future.

Our action is not an end in itself. We invite those who are ready to lay aside fear and economic addictions in order to join in the struggle: to confront injustice in words and deeds, to build a community worthy of men made in the image and likeness of God . . . a society in which it is easier for men to be human.

CHAPTER ONE

Judge Gordon had let me talk for five hours. He let me explain how I had become a "criminal" in the eyes of the law, how it could possibly be that I, a family man, would break into a federal building and burn selective service files. The date was March 20, 1970, the fifth day of the trial.

Five hours is a long time to talk. I knew I was "guilty" of the charges — that I was going to end up in jail. But it was exciting that I had this opportunity to go back over my life and over the dramatic action of the Milwaukee 14 which brought me to this witness chair in a federal court in Milwaukee.

The whole thing seemed incredible — and perhaps more incredible than anything was the fact that such a trial could still take place in America, that the judge was really letting me speak.

The prosecutor had asked Judge Gordon that I stop my narrative and that the usual question and answer period be followed. But Gordon had replied, "Well, this is the defendant and I am going to allow broad latitude in giving him his day in court."

And so I talked — as my thoughts came to me. My defense attorney Jim Shellow (Shellow, Shellow and Friebert) had refused to rehearse anything with me before. He wanted me spontaneous, the way I am. I looked out over the courtroom where my wife Netty and my three kids were listening and many, many other quiet, supporting friends in the peace movement, and I felt relaxed and deeply grateful, and the words came easily.

But it had to reach an end soon. I sensed Shellow was waiting for the precise dramatic moment.

Then barely audible in that terribly quiet room, came his final question:

"Michael, did you on September 24, 1968, intend to burn draft files and to hinder the administration of the Military Selective Service Act?"

The courtroom was even more still. My own heart — and mind — seemed to have been stilled too. This was it — but I hadn't even planned an answer to that question. I fully believe what Christ promised — that He would tell us what to say when we are dragged before tribunals.

After what must have seemed eternity to the others, I rose to my feet and without hesitation, loud and clear, said what was my final defense:

"I did what I did lest I be judged not a man but a coward. I did what I did even though I knew I jeopardized my wife's future and the future of my children. I did what I did even though I jeopardized a future in this society. But I stood with those other men on that day, on that evening, in that place, and at that time, lest I be judged less a man. I did it lest I be condemned. And so I stand before you. So God help me!"

Amazingly, the prosecutor had but one question. It was over.

And then began the long, tense wait. Netty and I took a walk expecting to be called back quickly. Shellow and everyone else thought the verdict would come within the hour. But the hour passed and another, then five hours, ten hours, and almost eleven. Could this really be? Could it be that someone on that jury was really doubting my guilt? Shellow had built the entire case around my intent and my compulsion to act out of religious conviction. Was there really someone on that jury who could not convict me for burning paper in protest of our government's burning, napalming men — women and children in Vietnam?

The jury was made up of nine women and three men. Gordon had allowed sixteen witnesses to testify in my behalf the day before. An incredible number of character witnesses! Did one of the skid row men, one of those who had come to the Casa Maria Catholic Worker House, get through to the jury — to one person on the jury? A Catholic priest had testified, and Bishop Buswell, a Roman Catholic bishop from Colorado. When asked what my reputation was in the community, Bishop Buswell answered (incredibly): "I think his reputation is that of a saint," and after a long pause, he emphasized it by, "That's S A I N T, saint!" Wild. Was there a Roman Catholic on that jury who could not send a man to jail whose reputation, according to the testimony of a bishop, was that of a saint?

But after the long wait, the jury reached the inevitable verdict. It must have been around 11 p.m. A hundred or more people had been waiting quietly with vigil candles outside the federal court building. Many of them had been with me the whole trial. When the word spread that

15

the verdict was ready, they, too, knew the inevitable. But they filed into the courtroom sending me their quiet support by humming very softly, "Michael Row Your Boat Ashore."

The jury came in, tired, expressionless. I felt a pang of sadness for these men and women who had had to give up their time and who had had to bear such a burden — judging a man's guilt.

The judge asked. The word came. "Guilty."

I arose and thanked the jury and apologized for taking much of their time. I thanked the judge and told him I thought he was a good man. I thanked the marshalls for doing their job well. And I thanked my friends for their quiet and respectful support.

The action of the Milwaukee 14 had received a lot of publicity, just as we intended. But the trial, too, received wide coverage and to many it was a sign of hope in these seemingly hopeless times. Many people began asking for transcripts of my testimony. In effect, they were asking me for my life story. They were perplexed (hopefully) as to what led me to what I am and to what I did. How was it that a traditional Irish Catholic, just twenty-eight years old, a former seminarian for the Catholic priesthood, an alien still in love with this country he had lived in for only nine years, a husband and father of three young children, a success-ful (for whatever that means) insurance salesman, had become such a "law-breaker"?

Many in the city of Milwaukee and in the country thought the world had gone mad, that surely the men like the Milwaukee 14 were madmen. Yet they knew that the people involved in the blood-pouring and napalming of draft files out East and those in Milwaukee were not criminal types, that they were not doing something for kicks or for self-profit, that they were not uneducated slobs or dropouts, but often intelligent, educated men. Catholic priests were among them.

Some of my closest friends, my family, wanted an explanation. And I knew they deserved one. If it had only involved myself — but a wife and three children!

The transcript of the trial tells a lot. But there's much more. More details, deeper details. The careful planning, for example, of the action itself, the way it was agreed it had to be carried out — totally in a non-violent manner.

The danger of telling the story is that it may look as if I am trying to sell Michael Cullen. All I can give you is my word — that this is not the case.

I write first of all to explain to my loved ones whom I may have hurt, in some hope that they will understand and not be disillusioned by what I did.

16

Secondly, if I can in some small way contribute to peace, if I can in some small way change the insane direction of this great country, if I can in some small way influence my brothers and sisters in the revolution movement to see that non-violence is the only way, then these chapters are a worthwhile effort.

But perhaps the greatest contribution that I as a Christian can offer is hope. Perhaps I can offer some hope to the many who are despairing, to the young and old who no longer wear smiles on their faces. I will not say that only the Christian can dance and sing before a world gone mad with power and destruction, but dance and sing we must or we, too, will lose our sanity in an insane society, where suppression, guns, bombs — death — is the only "solution" to a dying species.

The Christian knows the answer to death is not more death but a celebration of life. And even if he is thrown into jail, tossed to the lions, gassed and tear-bombed, and even if he should lose his very life in the process, he knows with absolute certitude that his suffering and death is redemptive and that he is winning.

Our times are grave, perilous, and we stand on the brink of total death and destruction. Perhaps then, more than at any time in history, it is a time to dance, a time to sing, a time to celebrate the beauty and sacredness and wonder and mystery of who we are and what we are and why we are. It is a time to celebrate life.

Am I just a wild-eyed dreamer? Has the insanity of our times and of our people afflicted me also?

Let me begin where I began — back in Ireland.

CHAPTER TWO

But like in many Irish families, you know, I don't even really know where I was born. They never tell you much when you're growing up. There is a whole mystique about being born that is definitely cultural. As far as I know, I was born in my father's house just outside the village of Ashford which is north of Wicklow in County Wicklow on the southeast coast of Ireland.

I was born on November 8, 1941, the fifth of nine children. There are three older brothers, Oliver, Liam and Dan, and one older sister, Maeve. After me there are Joan, Finton, Frank and Maureen.

My mother, Mary Elizabeth Dunne, was born in Los Angeles and she was one of two children. My grandmother on my mother's side had come to the United States around 1912. She met my grandfather in the States. They were married here and I believe my mother was no more than three years of age when they decided to go back to Ireland. My grandfather then bought a farm in the County Wicklow. There my mother was raised and her brother Mike was born.

Uncle Mike went to study for the priesthood. He had joined the White Fathers and went to Africa to continue his studies for the priesthood. He had been ordained a deacon, the last step before the Catholic priesthood when the Nazis came. He was placed in a concentration camp and suffered immensely. This has played a real role in my mother's reaction to my going to jail. My relatives had to get the Irish government to show that Uncle Mike wasn't an English citizen.

He came back to Ireland a very broken man and it took him quite a few years to recuperate. He never was ordained a priest and he never married. He lives in England now, very much alone.

18

But again they never told us young kids much. For example, my grandfather's American experiences are very mysterious. I know he crossed the Atlantic a number of times with my mother and my grandmother staying in Ireland. He finally stayed in Ireland. For his last ten years, he was an invalid — but much of his problem was mental, I think. Culturally it is interesting how the Irish viewed mental illness. Mental illness was held against a family, as something not to be proud of.

The same kind of shame would come to one who began studying for the priesthood and didn't make it. For me to go back to Ireland immediately after leaving the seminary would have been rough because the people would have considered me a failure, and psychologically it would have been too hard. But I wanted to live in the States anyhow. If I'm deported now (which is still a possibility) after all I've come through, I would have no problem and would probably join Bernadette Devlin.

The Irish are a proud people and their struggle to be free over the centuries has given them a fierce determination. Defeat and failure are not part of their vocabulary, and even when it happens, it is not discussed openly. As we'll see, I was written off as a failure at age fifteen for not doing what I set out to do. Sometimes I think only my mother has kept confidence in me.

My mother, then, was raised in Ireland. I think she wanted to become a nun at one time. She is a great singer. She has a marvelous voice, and was trained by the guy who trained John McCormick. She sang in many operas and was planning to come to the States to sing when she met my father. I think my mother's in her late fifties now, but that's another thing. They never told us their ages. I once asked my grandmother her age and she snapped at me with tremendous rage and booted me in the rear. My father's sixty-eight, but I just discovered that recently. I'm not sure of his birthday, though. I don't even know my mother's birthday. They'd never tell you that. I know they were married in 1936, so they must have told us that. But I'm not sure of the exact date.

But I remember hearing my mother sing at home and at weddings. What a tragedy that so much talent was not used. Ireland has a history of such suppressions — perhaps mainly because it is so culturally tied to the Church where the role of women is minimal. That's why Devlin is so significant. She is moving Ireland to a whole new social awareness of women and their future roles in society — call it women's liberation, if you like. In Ireland these women need a lot of liberating.

These apparently small things are lasting experiences. They are impacts on my life and there's no way of articulating how I feel because they play such a mystery. Why were my parents and teachers afraid to speak about the Irish civil war? Is this shaded Irish history the same as the shaded American history taught in this country? I think so.

19

The Irish school system did little educating. There was a lot of emphasis on the classics, but there was nothing very scholarly about it, nothing creative about it. There was great emphasis on memorization. We memorized classic poetry, for example, but no room was left for creativity.

I sort of rebel at so much of my youth. Although I never was taught racism, it all seems to me to fit the same picture and I can understand Bernadette Devlin when she talks about the false Christianity of Ireland. For example, she talks about the false Christianity of a small town. Gossip groups, you know, and not getting down to the heart of what the faith is all about. Though our country was littered with graveyards of martyrs and holy places, there was much more emphasis on the Church as institution than there was on the Christian faith. Though Ireland is well known for its missionaries and its great scholars, or at least scholars of the faith, there's still something rotten about it that evades real Christian formation. Like the Irish who come to this country. How many end up as racists? How many end up as exploiters? The country's filled with them. Many Irish immigrants in New York City are racists. They couldn't begin to put it together. Now maybe they will, with the help of someone like Devlin.

My mother's people were from the deep South. They were from a place called County Kerry and there were a lot of priests in her family and that gave them some kind of status.

There was also a great mystery on my father's side. He was born in the mountains, one of seven children, very poor. He was much older than my mother and came from a very poor farm which was mostly stones. His father was an alcoholic and died on the way home one day. There was never much said about him except he was called Red Cullen. My father's mother raised the kids. None of those children got much of an education. They walked seven or eight miles down the mountains to get to this convent school. My father got what might be the equivalent of an eighth grade education.

But I want to stress that the poverty was real. When you talk about Ireland twenty-five or thirty or forty years ago, you are talking about incredible poverty.

I think it important that I was raised on a farm, a moderately wealthy farm in Ireland, but a primitive farm by American standards. I was raised on a farm where we threshed our meal, a farm like people in the 1800's or 1900's would talk about. Just as Peter Maurin could talk about the peasants of France, I in 1970 can talk about my own life time and I'm only twenty-eight years of age. Ireland has become somewhat mechanized, but I remember cutting the oats with the scythe and the binder.

My father was a hard worker. When he left school, he went down

20

from the mountains and brought his sheep with him. He had raised the sheep, about a thousand of them, on the wide open country on the mountains. He made some money when he sold his sheep and with it he started a business as a butcher. He bought a van (and at that time an automobile was rare in Ireland), and he used it as a traveling butcher. He went around to all the farmers in the whole large county of Wicklow. He bought and sold eggs and sold meat to the farmers who didn't butcher themselves.

This is how he met my mother. She had a high school education and was considered an upper middle class person. He was considered lower class, even though he was a butcher.

There was a tremendous class division even then, a form of racism. It's really the same thing in Ireland today and it keeps coming out. It's not basically a Protestant-Catholic problem, but an economic problem, a social-economic problem which is really three or four centuries old in Ireland.

The Irish Revolution didn't change anything. The best men in Ireland were shot in 1916. Oppression merely changed hands. The power remained in the hands of a few. The mentality never changed. The caste system still exists. Little has changed in Ireland.

Another reason why my father was in a lower class in Ireland was because he had no relatives who were priests or religious. But my mother had an uncle who was a priest and so she was in a privileged class.

But what Ireland and my parents and grandparents really gave me is the faith. My faith has meant so much. The priesthood was so obviously the best place you could be of service to mankind. This has all kinds of cultural and spiritual implications. I think there were many frustrated vocations. It wasn't just a matter of not being a priest. It was just that you weren't able to serve the faith which was so important to you. There weren't structures in lay society in which or by which you could really serve the fullness of the Gospel.

I guess that's the reason why we haven't had any real heroes in Ireland in the lay state as of late, except people like our alchoholic friend from Dublin, Matt Talbot. I think this explains the tremendous growth of the Legion of Mary in Ireland. It was the first Church movement in which lay people could express their faith. As I look back now, I think there was too much emphasis on doctrine and on getting people into the Church or back to the Church to save their souls. The Legion of Mary was not a Christianity that really deals with social ills and social solutions, but it was an outlet for lay people.

That's why I think I'm very fortunate to have come to the States the way I did. The thing that really comes across in my youth is the

21

emphasis on faith and this faith still permeates my life today in everything I do. It is the reason why I can stand in times when others may despair. Credo — I believe. I keep saying it in Latin, but no matter what language you say it in, it comes across. Credo — I still believe in the faith. I'm sometimes afraid to say that out of fear that men won't believe me. Because of my faith I almost welcomed jail as a new way of dying to get into something that I know has to happen — for the Church and also for this society. I had fears, yes, and I knew the kind of brutality that goes on in our jails which is much more psychological than it is physical. I welcomed the opportunity, even though I was walking away from my family. It was much more important to face the situation, even alone, and to be strengthened by what I am becoming and what my family is becoming because I am not with them.

It is the faith which gives me strength and will see me through. I can never give thanks enough for the faith. Ireland was like one big seminary. It was all so very real. Ireland was full of people preparing to be missionaries and there were hundreds of missionaries returned to Ireland, relating their exciting experiences in spreading the faith in foreign lands.

No wonder Ireland has so many vocations. It's like being in the army, you eat and sleep the thing. I question sometimes whether it is faith or Ireland's culture that is operating. Yet, I want to emphasize the thanks that I have for my faith, despite the inhumanity of the Church as an institution. Even though the Church has been corrupted and I know it still is in terms of institution and corporation, there's still some mysterious thing, a mystery that I do love.

Maybe that's vague, but I wouldn't want to try to clarify it. The faith, after all, is mystery. In Ireland, the faith was paid for by martyrs. The Irish martyrs are not merely something cultural. These men and women did die for their faith. My grandmother on my mother's side used to speak about the 1840 famine. She talked about people giving up their faith for a bowl of soup. There were soup lines that were supplying bread to people who would give up their faith. But many people, true martyrs, starved to death for their faith. This is an incredible part of Irish history, that suffering, that tremendous suffering they endured, that does come across no matter how you break it down. That still lives with us. It's very real. These martyrs were much like the early Christians, and we're inheritors of this history of the Church.

(I always like to think of the United States in the 1840's as the hospitality house of the world. It was the one place where people could come who were running away from tyranny, from exploitation, who were running away from religious domination or religious persecution, who could find a home, who could find a new place; where people could begin to build a future for themselves and prevent from happening what drove them from their home countries.

Of course, this is definitely related to the draft too. You find the emigrants from Europe were often running away from draft systems. Most people don't know about the anti-draft riots in New York City — 1200 people were murdered. Many of these were Irish running away from tyranny in Ireland as a result of English domination there.)

But the Irish of the twenty-six counties of the South then and now are so tied to the Catholic Church. The religious thing has always been there. And even now, after 2000 years we are left with this great mystery which I think we can rebuild. That hope I still have and that's the hope I want to be able to transmit to our young people. I'm not just some mysterious character who has come out of this heritage. The faith itself is truly rich. And though I think we'll take on totally new directions in the future, hopefully we'll learn from the cultural problems that the Church had when it got too tied in as it did in Ireland, when it got related with the people in power and when the Church started walking hand in hand with the executives in power. That's when the Church really begins to lose its emphasis and its reality and its presence. But the Church is a sign of life and of hope. This is all part of my mystery.

All of this comes to bear on how people must look at what I am doing now. Some people worry about who our enemy is. I don't worry about that. I don't worry about who is infiltrating, even though I know there are infiltrators. Because faith goes much deeper than that. They can throw us into jails and persecute us and bring false witnesses against us. This is happening. I don't mean to make myself another Christ or a saint. But I know I'm doing the right thing. This is the history I come out of. This is the fact of my faith. This is the heritage of my mother and my father, my family, though poor they were. There were class distinctions which I think have to disappear and have to be worked out and have to be thought about, but something much deeper was operating — the faith.

It was in 1930 that my father bought a house, the house in which I was raised. That was in a place called Kiltymon. The village has become known as Coynes Cross and that's where my family is still living. The highway passes right by the house and I am afraid the highway will be widened and the house may have to be removed. At that place we have about ten or twelve acres of land. My sister Maureen, the youngest in the family, has opened a "Spinning Wheel," a kind of gift shop, tea stop, to entertain Americans. She has a little business going.

Some things stand out in my youth that were very important. Prayer is one thing. Even though I wasn't a religious nut in some form, prayer was there, always. I remember working on the farm, in the field, making hay — and praying all the while. Not because I wanted to be religious. It was a great gift of the faith that I knew was not just mine. I'd leave early in the morning to get to Mass. It was not an obligation. I always felt that I would get the benefit of this sometime in my life. It wasn't a matter of salvation but it had some real purpose to it. It's hard to talk about it. It's easy for someone to think I have a swelled head. But these things operated very powerfully and they are real landmarks in my life.

For example, when I was only sixteen I went to a place called Lough Derg in the mountains of Donegal, where you go for three days of fasting and prayer in memory of St. Patrick who fasted there for forty days. There was always an emphasis on fasting. When I had a difficulty in this country, the first thing I would do is fast — not because Ghandi did it — I hadn't even read the life of Ghandi — it was because of my heritage. I understood fasting as a means to bring spiritual power to solve problems that I didn't understand.

Anyway, this pilgrimage became a real part of me. I wanted to go to this island at that particular time because it was the anniversary year of St. Patrick — when the faith was brought to Ireland. Once I left home I began fasting, and I had to go 250 miles to this island by train and then went on the island. Once on the island, pilgrims would take off their shoes and in bare feet, fast and pray for three days. Once a day the pilgrims were allowed to have black toast and black tea.

What really struck me at Lough Derg was the faith. Thousands of people came to the island that weekend. There's a small cathedral there, really just a big chapel, where you can pray, make the Stations of the Cross or listen to sermons being given on various aspects of the Church, on the faith. And that goes on all the time — all night. You stay up for the first forty-eight hours. You sleep only one night of the three days on the island. So you are really in for some penance.

This is very hard to talk about because it so much goes against our culture here in the States. The whole emphasis on faith is lacking in the States. Do we really believe in the Incarnation? Do we really believe that things did change at the Incarnation? Do we really believe that here in the States? Are we really afraid of the word "martyrdom"? Not that we become martyrs for the sake of our head, but do we really understand that the total Christian gives totally?

People don't even understand in my own neighborhood in the Casa Maria community. We're sharing everything in common and we're not afraid and there's a point at which we are willing to die. Some people simply don't understand that because it's totally against America's culture. Prayer and penance are not in line with this culture. This culture is materialistic. That is why, for example, people cannot understand the

24

simple philosophy of a Catholic Worker house like Casa Maria. When a man is hungry, feed him. Because it's the right thing to do and it's the most obvious thing to do.

I was almost trapped into this materialistic culture. If I hadn't moved when I did, I may never have moved.

But the emphasis on faith, on prayer, on penance, on repentance — this is all a part of me from experiences like Lough Derg. Nor was this all just a personal thing. There was a lot of prayer for the needs of others, for the needs of Ireland and of the people of the world, for the suffering of the world. This was all emphasized.

(There was another place called Croagh Patrick in the west part of Ireland, in the County Mayo — I pilgrimaged there in May of 1961, just before I came to the United States. St. Patrick came to Ireland in 432 as a slave. He fed pigs in the mountains of County Antrim and later got back on a ship to France, where he was ordained. Then he came back to preach the message of Jesus to the people of Ireland. And so, Ireland became a Christian nation from the fifth century on.

Anyway, St. Patrick fasted on this high mountain that comes out of the ocean called Croagh Patrick. People have been pilgrimaging there for centuries in the spring of the year. They walk up the mountain in bare feet, and they do what we call the Stations of the Cross, the fourteen signs that lead to Christ's death — you know, his agony in the garden, his scourging at the pillar, Pontius Pilate's act of condemning him, the nailing of the cross, his death, taking his body down from the cross and the burial of Jesus — signs and meditations that go along with what happened in the death of Christ. On your way up this mountain, which, of course, is supposed to symbolize Calvary, where Christ was crucified, you meditate. The pilgrims start in the early evening and walk all night into six o'clock in the morning. The top of this mountain is always covered with mist, covered with clouds, and there is a small chapel. It has happened that people have fallen off the mountain. The Irish have funny names for that kind of death. It's a good way to death, falling off a holy mountain.

There's a story about St. Kevin, for example, a saint of the sixth century. Some woman was supposed to be after him. St. Kevin felt he'd never make it to heaven if his lover kept after him. She was a detriment to his soul and so he pushed her off the mountain. She landed in the lake and as far as I know she's still there. The Irish have a strange sense of humor. I don't mean it to be irreverent. I just think it's funny.

On top of the mountain, people pray, Mass is offered, and the pilgrims come back down the mountain. This to me was a very important experience, the faith — the faith again — the faith of the people, the willingness to suffer physical suffering for the good of us all, something unheard of in these times.

25

To me, that's what going to prison is about. We knew we were going to get punishment of some type. But this had to be accepted out of love for people because we're in such terrible times. I think the people of Ireland were doing this, accepting punishment on themselves. Maybe punishment is not the best word. I don't know how to phrase it, except something is coming across there, a deeper interest in what was happening. That was in the people's lives, in their faces, in their eyes and hearts. That was very visible.

There's another place called Knock in County Mayo. Here is a different kind of setting. It's a more contemporary one. I think in the 1700's or 1600's — our Blessed Mother, the mother of Jesus, was supposed to have appeared to the village people. The village people were very simple people, people who had not much of an education. Education during the English domination was forbidden to the Irish, like it was in the South of this country to the blacks, who were not allowed to go to the best schools. You know, they were slaves. The Irish were like the black slaves of this country, forbidden by the same landlord, the English, from getting an education.

So, it wasn't until the 1800's, when the Irish finally began to get an education. We used to have in Ireland what was called the "hedge school." Teachers got educated in England, in France, somewhere on the continent, came back and would break the law in a sense because it was against the law to get an education and then to educate the Irish, who they called the "cabbage people" or "people of the fields." They would go down in the evening and hide behind the bushes and teach the people the language, how to read.

The people of the town of Knock were an example of simple people with little education. But the parish priest there had done something to protest. I can't recollect what it was — anyhow, I know he was going to be killed by some of the town's people. The Blessed Mother appears. These things — I don't understand — I don't know how to speak of them. Something did happen. The people said it happened, that the Blessed Mother did appear.

We used to make pilgrimages to that place, many times. We'd leave on Saturday night, on the train. Once we'd leave home, prayer and fasting would begin, all the way to Knock in the West of Ireland. It would take almost ten, twelve hours on the train. There we had prayer. Prayer was a real landmark, prayer, the rosary, the faith of the people of the Gaelic language, the simplest of people.

When I went to France in 1965, my wife and myself went to a place called Lourdes, where a similar thing happened, where our Lady is supposed to have appeared to St. Bernadette. And something — I don't know how to explain — I don't want to get mystical — except something

26

happened. A tremendous something happens to people's lives as a result of that happening with this young woman. There were people from all over Europe I met there, even Chinese, people from behind the Iron Curtain. And I found the same faith, the same extraordinary spirit. All night, we prayed.)

But praying all night was not an unusual thing for me. The house I grew up in was a house of prayer.

It was a big, wild house. There was no basement (Irish houses have no basements) and no central heating. We often had two blazing fires in the house, but it was still a cold house.

(Our kitchen had a dirt floor, clay, because we were poor. I remember raising baby lambs in the kitchen, next to the fireplace. In the cold winters, in the month of February, many sheep would begin to have lambs. Lambs often die of cold out in the mountains. So my father would bring the weak ones into the kitchen, because it was warm there, and there was no heat anywhere else.)

I remember when the kitchen was tiled. I was about twelve or fourteen when we got electricity and about fifteen when we put in an indoor toilet. The bathroom was another room they added on. They used to add on rooms as they needed them. We had nine kids in our family and the people used to say they would always know when Willie Cullen was going to have another baby — it was when he was adding another room on the house. For a while there were about six of us in one bedroom and then we built another room for the girls. Now there must be five bedrooms and a kitchen and dining room and a parlor.

Ireland gets very chilly, and wind gets icy. If Ireland didn't have the currents it would be a freezing country. It's a rainy and wet country. The dampness is incredible. We've got a lot of fog and we've got a lot of frost — mostly frost — heavy frost in Ireland.

Our only fuel at that time was turf or peat. We used to go into the mountains into what is called a bog, a damp and swampy place where a kind of moss grows. This moss dies every year and we used to cut it with a kind of spade and stack it on piles. It looks like wood after the summer dries it out, and then we used to get a donkey and cart and bring it down to the house and pile it up in the back of the house. My house is near a very small village, though perhaps it's grown into a nice village now. This was all about twenty-five miles out of Dublin, and, of course, to us it was like 300 miles. I didn't go to Dublin until I was nearly fourteen years of age.

Our diet was very simple. There were special days in the year that we used to eat special kinds of foods. On Sundays we always had a full course meal. This meant we had potatoes, vegetables, meat and then we had tea which was like coffee and then we had dessert which would be something sweet. I always loved the brown gravy my mother used to make. Even though we were butchers we ate meat only three times a week. Other families ate meat maybe once a week. We were butchers so we were much more fortunate.

After my father got married, he opened up a butcher business right there in the area, right next to our house, like a garage. He sold meat in the neighborhood and then he got himself a store, another butcher shop, in Bray, a village to the north, closer to Dublin. There he built a nice business. Right next to our house he built a shed which became a slaughter house. So I grew up in the slaughter house during most of my youth, killing cattle and sheep and pigs and so forth. We killed an average of three cattle a week and that was pretty good business. My father hadn't much of an education but he had a fantastic mind in terms of business. He was a great speculator and so he accumulated. He out-did anyone of his family — all his brothers and sisters.

My father was a very strict man. He was strict on all of us and he beat the hell out of us most of the time if we didn't do our job, our work. We all had to grow up with a certain kind of discipline, a kind of work. Work was almost child labor and too brutal sometimes. He used a stick from time to time or a strap or a kick in the pants. There was a lot of fear operating. We were all very afraid of my father. I could never talk with my father — about many things — even immediately prior to leaving for the U.S. Terrible discipline — terrible discipline.

(But it was through the efforts of my father, whom I appreciate now more fully than ever before because of his policies, that none of us children really ever suffered hunger or from the cold. He didn't let us get away with anything. Maybe he's why I am what I am now.)

My mother was the gentle part, of course. My mother was the part that made up for all the strictness of my father and, of course, this had played a great part in my life. She is such a gentle, such a noble woman, such a woman of prayer, and truly a really saintly woman and is today, very definitely. She is everything you think of when you think of a good Irish mother. She exemplifies everything that is beautiful. She stands as a real monument in my life.

My father had no use for education and I think it's because he never got it himself. Or maybe he just felt he'd done well without it and he saw a lot of educated idiots around who weren't doing what he thought was important. He never liked the government either. He felt the Irish government was taxing the people to death and he felt that Ireland was going down hill and not going anywhere.

But he was making a headway, a great headway, and in addition to his butchering business, he began acquiring more land, as much as 200 acres of it — which is a lot of land in Ireland. But as a result, my brothers knew nothing but work. There was very little time for my brothers to get an education. I was the first one that got a secondary education. My sister Maeve got a chance to go to secondary school, but she didn't like it after two years.

Part of the reason none of us like school is because our grade school experience was so bad. We used to walk four miles one way to grade school. I began walking there when I was three and a half years of age. That's when we started to go to school. It was a joke in many ways. Schools in Ireland were jokes. Granted we were in a very poor part of Ireland, in the mountains. The two teachers were two old maids. They were good people, but strict, Christian Brother style, who were free with corporal punishment. If you didn't learn the lessons, they beat the hell out of you, with a stick, cane and all.

(Corporal punishment was a very real part of my education, slaps on the legs and being hit with good scalpk thorns. The teachers would take one of the tree branches from the forest nearby, and they used this on our hands when we wouldn't read properly or wouldn't be learning one of our lessons, wouldn't be behaving properly.

And I remember one day, the teacher left the room, and one of the dunces was teaching. We used to call those who had special privilege with the teacher dunces. He was supposed to teach the class. Well, I brought in a water pistol, sat in the front row and took a spat at this guy. On the back of the board was some of the teacher's work, and the water destroyed all her work. I remember she brought me to the back of the room, and I got fifteen slaps. Incredible!)

The school had too many students, all poor students from around the neighborhood, the community. There were about one hundred, maybe more, in six grades. The two teachers had to teach everything.

Ireland had this mad disease of having to learn Gaelic, and if you didn't pass your Gaelic lessons you didn't pass anything. So much time was wasted. The Gaelic language had almost died. But we were all young children from the east coast of Ireland whose parents couldn't even speak Gaelic. Now on the west coast of Ireland many of the parents spoke Gaelic and so it was not very difficult for those kids to learn Gaelic. My father couldn't speak Gaelic. Wicklow is on the east coast, next to England and it was very anglicized. The English government had had its roots there since 1172. The only thing that was basic to us was our faith and a culture that was still preserved in the face of English imperialism, but the language truly had been changed. But the Irish government that had come in 1922 insisted that Ireland go back to its natural language as well as have the English language. So every school in Ireland had to teach Gaelic and you had to learn it. In fact they made it a law that if you didn't pass your last examination in Gaelic in high school, you

29

didn't pass anything. You didn't get certified. Crazy. This used to cause nightmares for the kids. More time was spent learning Gaelic than we spent on the subjects and a lot of other things we never learned. I never learned how to read properly until I was in high school.

I did learn a lot from the reading I did at home. My mother had kept a whole library that my grand uncle, the priest, had given her. But learning was de-emphasized in my family, mainly because my father saw how hard it was to make a living. Yet, we were a little more privileged than most. Most kids got no education. Most didn't even get a secondary education in Ireland. They just passed a law recently that made secondary education compulsory in Ireland. This would be somewhat equivalent to high school here, maybe even equivalent to one year of college.

The same exam for the whole of Ireland is given on the same days all over Ireland, for those who finished their first six years. This caused all kinds of cheating. People would try to get the exam ahead of time. Really incredible.

My mother had some education but it didn't play much of a role in forming us. We were struggling to make a living, struggling to stay alive.

A real childhood memory is Halloween. We used to go out like you do here, trick or treaters. But we didn't trick or treat anyone. We would go out with our talents and go to the neighbors and sing songs. We dressed up in all kinds of weird costumes and masks. We'd go all around the township and the whole countryside and each group would try to outdo the other. No one would ever know who was in whose band. We'd sing and dance to the accordion. We would knock on the door and the people would welcome us in and first everybody'd laugh at the costumes. Then we'd perform for our treats. There would be theatre groups and they'd sing songs and they'd dance, like the strolling minstrels. It was a great night of entertainment.

But little else happened in Ireland in my early youth. I didn't go to a movie until I was about fourteen — until I could ride a bicycle well. I had to ride a bicycle seven miles to see a movie.

Shrove Tuesday, the day before Lent, was a day of great festivities. It was the only time pancakes were served. You'd eat so many pancakes you'd be glad you couldn't eat anymore for another year.

We ate turkey on Christmas. As a kid I used to watch the turkey getting fat because that meant Christmas was getting close. There were so many things about Christmas. It was the food and the anticipation for it and the kind of poverty that would go on before it. And then the big banquet, and all kinds of parties. My relatives would invite us to their house.

The Christmas cake was special. My mother would bake it about seven weeks before Christmas. It was a fruit cake, made with a lot of whiskey, and it would be hanging somewhere aging. The plum puddings were also very special. They were made about the same time, seven or eight weeks before Christmas, and had a lot of whiskey and beer in them. And they would be aging and of course you would see them hanging around aging, and the anticipation was fantastic. Then we would go out into the woods to pick holly and ivy, singing seasonal songs all the while. Holly and ivy were an expression of Christmas. They were the only greens around at that time of the year. Holly, of course, has the red berries, and we would put them behind the picture of the Sacred Heart and other pictures.

The closer it got to Christmas, the more work we butchers had to do. My father would buy and kill as many as a hundred and fifty turkeys, and maybe even more than that — two or three hundred turkeys. And we had to pluck every one of those. I plucked turkeys as soon as I could pull a feather, and if I couldn't pull out the big feathers, I could pull out the little ones. We plucked them dry, and that was a hard task. We did the same to the chickens and ducks. Cleaning them was a big job. And also rabbits. That was a whole culture in Ireland. Many poor people lived on rabbits. Ireland was filled with rabbits! They were wild rabbits, and you'd go snaring them and trapping them. And there'd be some men, like you've often heard of — like your woodsmen and trappers in the early history of America — in Ireland there'd be these men like that, old men out in the woods, in the mountains, trapping rabbits. Sometimes they'd bring down fifty rabbits at a time to my father. My father would skin them and sell the skins and then he'd dress the rabbits and sell them in the store. So all this was part of Christmas.

There was the bringing of whiskey and the beer into the house. Some years ago, Father Matthew, a Franciscan from County Cork, started this movement — for the penance you would not drink, or you'd stay off alcohol, from the day you were confirmed until you were twenty-one years of age. Then perhaps you'd take the pledge for life. This was to atone for the sins that would be committed by the misuse of alcohol. Father Matthew called it "Reparation to the Sacred Heart."

But at Christmas time alcohol always appeared in the house, lots of alcohol. My father drank and drank but never drank to excess. He was always very careful, and my mother too. And we kids never touched it. There wasn't much drinking at all by the young people.

At Christmas time, of course, the Christmas crib was the big scene. We used to make candles in all different colors. These were big candles as tall as two or three feet. We would put them in the window on Christmas Eve. They'd scoop out a big turnip and put the candle in and stand it up. It would burn all Christmas as a sign that Jesus, Mary and Joseph were on their way to Bethlehem and that they were welcome at our house that night. Anybody who came, who needed a place to stay, was welcome to stay at our house that night. I remember people coming to the house.

My mother was a great friend of the "Tinkers." The Tinkers were the Irish gypsies, and my father used to cut her down for it. Most of the people who were making it in the world would never take them into their parishes. They'd come, the poorest kids in the world, you know, with no shoes in the middle of winter. They'd live out in caravans, on the side of the road, in tents. And at our house they knew my mother. There were all different kinds of tribes, a whole, distinct culture, similar perhaps to what we're getting into today with the Woodstock nation. Much like that.

I believe that these people were an outgrowth of the famine. There were Irish who travelled all over Ireland as a result of the famine, getting food, uprooted from their homes. The gypsies were a part of all this. There's a grand song about that, a song I used to love. It's called, "I'm a Freeborn Man of the Travelling People," and I often think of that because I think of Churches. That's what we should be — freeborn people, travelling people. Anyhow, my mother used to take in the Tinkers a lot and at Christmas time they'd be around, too, and they used to come in to mend pots and pans. But most of them she got to know as friends. They were poor people and my mother would feed them. They often ate at our table, though many of the Tinkers would be fed at the back door because of my father.

(All my youth, I remember the gypsies coming to the door at my home. My mother would never turn them away — never. And I guess it determines in part why I would never turn a person away from the doorway who comes for bread, food, or clothing. If I've got them, I give it to them. That's what it's all about, it seems to me. We are brothers and sisters of a common family. If we do not believe that, I fear for our future, for the future of this country and the world, for the future of man.

All this was a real part of my youth. The poor, the dispossessed of Ireland were always a part of my life. My mother would take them in. They would share the table with us. Often the people were barefooted, with ragged clothes they would have picked up second-hand, like the poor of our country today — the poor who get second-hand clothes, black poor, white poor, Chicano poor, and Indian poor and others — people in this society living on second-rate benefits. I saw this in my youth in Ireland. And we ourselves were poor at the time when these people were coming to our home.)

We often saw the skid row man too, the loner, the man of the road. These men were an important part of the youth, because I learned never to be afraid of the poor. My mother would give away anything, anything she had in the house. The last loaf of bread she'd give away. If my father found out, he would get angry. If he saw the beggars he would tell them to get a job or something like that. My mother did a lot of things behind my father's back. She helped a lot of people that he didn't know anything about. But my father did a lot of things behind my mother's back too, and behind all our backs. I know he used to send money for missions that no one ever knew was gone.

(Though my father was a tough man, a hard worker, hard on all of us, he was a religious man and not a flippant religious man. It wasn't something weightless. He was a man who knew what hard work was, knew what poverty was. But he knew how to pray — pray. It wasn't an extraordinary thing to see my father kneeling down at nighttime and praying because everything depended on providence in his mind: the raising of his children, the providing of food, the farm life.)

The rosary was the most important. He would always join us in the rosary which we prayed every night as long as I can remember. My mother felt that things were breaking up if we weren't saying the rosary. My mother would say we were losing our faith if we missed a day or so of saying the rosary. So we'd all try to be there for the rosary.

My mother had varicose veins and open ulcers on her legs. As long as I remember she has endured tremendous suffering, and still does. She always offered up her sufferings. She was always offering things up for the poor souls in purgatory and for the sufferings of the world. She was living the hard kind of life. She was always praying and making novenas, although she wasn't just a novena woman. She was really a woman of faith. She never was a hypocrite.

My mother is trying to understand what I'm doing now and she's probably the only one who really understands me. She can at least say that I'm doing what I want to do. She worried a lot about me for a while there. She didn't hear from me for a long time because I didn't know how to write to my family about it. I know it would be impossible to explain but now I think she begins to understand. She still fears a lot, as any mother does about her children and my children.

We did send clippings from time to time to the family. My brothers really don't understand. They think I should render to Caesar what is Caesar's and I told them sometimes when Caesar decides to look like God you don't render it to him. When Caesar decides to take things that are God's, you don't render it to him. But my brothers have made it now. Economically they've made it. My brothers are in business and are doing well and it is easy to forget the poor — whether they be immediately around you or they be in Southeast Asia.

33

There's another childhood experience that made a lasting impression. Perhaps it has something to do with my fear and hatred of war. I remember one Sunday when I was wearing a sailor suit playing in our yard between big piles of hay. I distinctly remember the sound of airplanes. The fear must have been tremendous because I didn't really understand. But I still have a vision of the airplanes passing high overhead. I couldn't have been over three, but I know what I was wearing and I saw the planes.

They told me when I grew up that the Germans bombed the cheese factory in Wexford and some factories in Dublin. Ireland was neutral, but Germany said that this was a mistake, that they thought they were bombing Liverpool. But Ireland was feeding the English by means of the cheese factories. The bombing was no mistake.

Then there was also at that time the rumor that Hitler planned to invade England, to box in England, and he was to land on the east coast of Ireland and to attack England from that side. Again a tremendous fear was operating because I remember my father talking about this. My father had some land right by the ocean on the east coast of Ireland. They had to fill all their fields up with carts of all kinds and barrels and anything to prevent the German planes from landing. Of course, it was like primitive people acting against a highly civilized technocracy. The Vietnamese are doing the same thing. It wasn't realistic. I'm sure the Germans would have found some way of landing. But Germany decided to go against Russia instead of coming through Ireland and the whole scene changed.

I was one in the family who could sing pretty well. My mother taught me a number of songs, mostly Irish rebellion songs and songs about the history of Ireland. And there was this one song called, "Boolvough." That was the name of an Irish town in County Wexford. Father Murphy was the leader of a community there and he always preached to the Irish not to rebel. Of course, the Church always did that. The Church always played hand and hand with the people in power, in this case, the English. Perhaps that was out of fear for the safety of their people but perhaps it was all part of the same exploitation. There were rebellious priests, but Father Murphy wasn't one of them. Perhaps he saw too many people die. Anyhow, one morning his church was burnt down to the ground. And that's when he became a rebel.

The sign of the Irish revolution was lighting the heather. This was the sign to the people that the revolution was on. There was a revolution in Ireland's history almost every twenty-five years, trying to seek freedom — or at least a few times every one hundred years. I mean a real revolution that went into the history books, a real mass mobilization of men and arms — the pikes, the hay forks, primitive weapons.

Anyway I always had a great love for the song about Father Murphy, a fine air. And every year there was this Feast of Music held in the village about three miles away in a place called Newtownmountkennedy. There was a Feast of Music during the summer in many different villages in every county. All the talent of the community which might be a whole county, maybe two counties, would come into the village. The Feast of Music would always be held in the open air. A field near the village would be rented or given and usually freely to the Feast of Music. There would be a tug of war and games for the men, but its main emphasis was on the music and the culture. Some trucks, lorries as we would say, would be brought in and on the backs of the lorries they would set up a stage and there the young people would come in their costumes and dance. Some of the old men and women would be the judges of the talent. The singers would sing songs. Some would play mouth organs and fiddles. Silver medals were given as prizes.

Well, my family was out visiting the holy places during that holy year and I was supposed to care for the farmyard, to milk our one cow, etc. But I wanted to go sing songs at the festival. So I put on my first pair of long trousers, because wearing long pants was the sign of being a man. I must have been about thirteen, but my corduroy pants were big for me. So I tied them up with twine string, hopped on my bicycle and headed for the festival. I entered my name in the contest and sang this song about Father Murphy. I got first prize.

I came home and my father was mad. He didn't ask where I was — he just beat the hell out of me. I'll never forget my father's boot in the back side and I usually generally ended up urinating in my pants half way on my way to the bed. Usually he'd make you go to bed and you wouldn't eat for a day, maybe longer. Real punishment. There was no time to tell them I had won the prize. But, I came down sheepishly at night time carrying the medal in my hand and great forgiveness was had and a lot of repentance and so forth, because they were very happy that I'd won this prize.

I used to sing at concerts and since my friend, Father Grogan, had a great interest in drama, I did some acting and was always singing Irish songs. We used to have a group that would go from village to village on the weekends giving concerts and singing songs and dancing.

So it was a very rich education outside of the classroom. The only thing we lacked was the skills that were required in education. Emphasis in Irish education was on this classroom lecture thing and if you weren't fortunate enough to get that you were bankrupt. Many kids never made it. I knew kids in Ireland who were smart as hell, whips, whose fathers were in the lower class, economically, and never got a chance for education. Some never even finished grade school. What a tragedy! But this is a world scene. We just take it for granted here, although here, too, there is a lack of creativity.

So just a couple of us went on to school. I got the chance because I wanted to become a priest. I was about eleven or twelve when I finally wanted to become a priest. Once I made that known, everything was prepared for me. I got all the chances. I guess I wasn't aware of that too much except that it was happening. But my education in grade school was so bad that no one thought I could make it in high school.

(I went to high school, what we call "secondary school," in the town of Wicklow, seven miles from my home, at the Christian Brother school. I rode a bicycle to high school, seven and a half miles one way. School started about 8:30 in the morning, but we all had what you call in this country chores to do before school, work to be done. We had to milk the cow, or feed the chickens, or drive in the cattle to be slaughtered that day or some other farm work before going off to school. It was always a tough job to get your lessons done, and our lessons were never thought of as very important by my father. My mother was different. She was the one who made sure we got our lessons in. This was pretty much the first thirteen or fourteen years of my life.)

I began to realize that with my educational background, I could never think of becoming a priest.

(I knew I wouldn't meet the requirements of most seminaries. And so, I thought I would become what is called a "brother," which is not necessarily secondary to a priest even though at that time, it was thought to be. Many brothers were much more religious men than some of the priests and bishops. But many brothers did manual work, with their hands. I decided I would be a carpenter and go to Africa and be a missionary. At least I could build churches.

A missionary in Ireland meant this: not one who went to spread the gospel and came back home. A missionary in Ireland meant you went to a country, and you took on all that country was and its heritage and culture and people, and you never thought of ever returning to your native land again. That's how I embraced this country. I came as a missionary to America, but I came because I wanted to be here. I wanted to be in the diocese of Pueblo, wanted to be in the people of this land, embrace it as your fathers or grandfathers and great grandfathers embraced this nation. They wanted to build a new society. To me, that's a missionary. That's a real missionary. A missionary embraces the people and never thinks of returning again.

So at that time I decided I would become a missionary brother — at age fifteen. So, I went to a place called Roxpershire in southern Scotland, to join the White Fathers. That's a strange name, but the White Fathers were a group of priests that came out of North Africa to be missionaries throughout the African continent in the late 1700's, early 1800's. There were a lot of Irish priests who had joined them.

The Irish have a heritage, a tremendous background and history as missionaries. From the fourth century on, Ireland was noted for its missionaries. The Dark Ages in Europe, for example, when the glow of freedom, of being free men and women on the Continent of Europe, no longer existed, it was the monasteries of Ireland — Benedictine, Trappist, Cistercian — that preserved Western civilization. It wasn't until about the eleventh century, when England invaded in 1172, that many monasteries were burned.

Again, the light of freedom was alive in the continent of Europe as a result of missionaries, people like St. Gall, who set out to a part of Switzerland and opened up monasteries which were places of education, places of learning. A monastery wasn't just a place where people got away from the real world. It was a place of bringing the best things of the world and making them a part of your life. You know, like what St. Benedict says, balancing your life is the greatest task, balancing life in terms of work, fasting and prayer, in terms of learning, knowledge, and work with your hands.

You find these monasteries even today throughout the world, like the Trappist monastery at Gethsemane, Kentucky, where Thomas Merton was. All of Western civilization owes a debt to the monks because they were people who preserved the wisdom of the early Fathers of the Church, the thought of Greek men like Plato and Aristotle, these men who influenced this country's heritage and other countries throughout the European Continent and Western world.

Irish monks trained the missionaries who went to the Continent of Europe and preserved freedom. The White Fathers were missionaries in that spirit.

I joined them in early 1957, but I didn't stay too long. Even though I was only fifteen I knew that I wanted to be more than the builder of churches and buildings. I wanted to be a man who could preach the gospel — a priest.

The people, of course, in my home town said: "Oh, he couldn't make it!" That was sort of the slap in the mouth, saying: "You didn't have the courage, Cullen." I said to myself that by God, if I ever go again to do what I wanted to do, I'd never return till I got what I wanted, what I wanted to be. So, that was an important mark.)

That taunting increased my desire to become a priest. I didn't know how I was going to do it, but I also knew I was good at a lot of things. I was good at the things that I enjoyed doing. I was a good talker, I was a good debater. Even in grade school I knew I could express myself well. I had done fairly well in some subjects like English and history and things like that. I had a very inquisitive mind — I was always asking questions. When I couldn't understand something I asked questions. Some of the teachers didn't like that — even here in America.

I feel I never got educated until after I left the seminary in America. I used to hate school in America, too. I felt that the subjects were so dry and irrelevant. It all was too mechanical, a very uncreative education. I resented education. I resented the way subjects were taught. When I took a course from a teacher who was really exciting, who really had something to give I always did well in it. But in high school and in college in this country I was a good debater because I read a lot outside of the classroom on my own.

Anyway I got the chance to become a priest primarily through our priest, Father Tom Grogan. He was a great and beautiful gentleman, a real human being, the best parish priest we ever had in our community, a good man, a saintly man, I will say that Father Tom Grogan had, outside of my mother, more influence on my early life than anybody else. He liked me and it wasn't simply because I wanted to become a priest. He liked me as a friend, and I loved him as a friend. We used to sing a lot together. He was the kind of guy who was always at odds with the bishop. For example, one day Tom Grogan told the archbishop of Dublin that he should never have been a priest, should never have been ordained. Tom Grogan was a man who thought for himself and Tom Grogan was hoping the day would come when he could get married. He was an old man and he was always saying that Pope John was going to change that celibacy thing. That was even before I was in the seminary.

I saw Tom Grogan for the last time when I went home in 1965. He died a few months after of cancer. He was a man of tremendous imagination. He wrote poetry and songs and he sang well and he could play the fiddle and the mouth organ, and the piano. He was a painter and a photographer — very creative and he loved traveling.

Tom Grogan got me into Roscrea because he knew a priest there at the Trappist monastery. Roscrea is the name of the town, St. Joseph's monastery was the name of the school. This was in the central part of Ireland, in the County of Tipperary, right in the plains of Ireland. I went there in April of 1957, very shortly after I came back from Scotland.

St. Joseph's is extraordinary and unusual compared with most monasteries. Unlike the early heritage of Ireland's history when monasteries were centers of education, most monasteries were no longer being used as centers of education, but now were centers of prayer and study, limited to the monks themselves. They were centers of contemplative prayer, meaning silence and prayers, like the Divine Office. Praying the Divine

Office is still part of my life. I still pray the psalms of the Old Testament. These psalms were and are sung in Gregorian chant by the monks in the monasteries throughout the world.

Roscrea was unusual because it was in Ireland where the monks provided education for outsiders, for men who did not intend to be monks. Roscrea had a college attached to it, what we call a college. Really it was a high school with maybe the equivalent of two years of college in the United States. I became a student there in 1957.

I didn't have sufficient money to go there, of course. The money was raised by Father Tom Grogan, the parish priest, and my family. Like most Catholic educational institutions, only people with money can make use of them. It's unfortunate because education by the Church should be for the common person, the poor and dispossessed, the people not able to get to other colleges. The poor of Milwaukee should be going to Marquette, for example. The poor of the neighborhood in Ireland should have been going to Roscrea. I was in essence becoming a part of the gentry in Ireland, the granted people, being educated, people making money. That's what this education was.

But Roscrea monastery did have a tremendous impact on people's lives, regardless of who they were or how they got there, and so has a deep influence in Ireland. A lot of young men were trained as missionaries there as well as for high positions as lawyers, doctors or influential people who have kept Ireland moving toward the future.

There were many studying to be priests in my class. Becoming a priest was an option, and many in my class did become priests. I studied there for three and a half years and hence, Roscrea had a tremendous impact on me. The college is right beside the monastery. The monastery has a kind of wall around it to show the sense of contemplativeness and quiet, silence. The monks don't speak except in times of classes and once in a while in recreation. The prayer life, the songs, the sense of understanding of what monasticism meant was deeply embedded in my life in those three and a half years. In fact, I don't think I could ever adequately describe them because they were an experience which had to be lived.

Some people ask, "Why do you still read the psalms?" Even though the Church is sort of breaking up today in the form that we've known it to be — the Roman Catholic Church. It's something embedded in your head and your bones. You can't get it out even though the structures are breaking up.

I look at Thomas Merton, for example, the Trappist monk who influenced this century probably more than most men. Thomas Merton was in Gethsemane, Kentucky. He was a convert to the Church, who wrote many books like *The Seven Storey Mountain and Faith and Violence*. At the time of his death, he was trying to link Eastern monasticism with

Western monasticism. He had gone to Bangkok and was killed accidentally by electric shock while he was taking a bath. A terrible tragedy. He was a young man who felt the monasticism of the future, of the next twenty years, would enter into the heart or into the bowels of this society so that men and women are not brutalized but are treated like brothers, so that we can resurrect the soul of society by being man.

But let me make myself clear. When I say these things, I am not judging anyone. Judgment is only in our own heads. We make judgments upon our own lives because it is no one man that is responsible for history. We all are responsible for history and to me that is the heart of the message of monasticism, that our lives are so central to changing things. Everyone of us, be we judges, be we jury, be we people in the audience, lay people, be we doctors or lawyers, whoever we may be, politicians or bishops, you know. Each one of us must uphold the sense of human, the sense of person as the most sacred part of changing history.

I think maybe that is what we are finding out today as a people in this society, that we *can* make the American dream come true if we decide to make it come true. That means every single last one of us. That means the most inarticulate of us, the poorest of us, the most educated of us. And we have responsibility to the extent that we have been given privilege. If we have been educated, we have privilege because there are many of our brothers and sisters around the planet, around this country, of all races and all denominations, who have not had the chance that some of us have had. But because we have had a chance and responsibility, there lies our judgment.

And to me that is what monasticism is all about. That is reckoning with what man and what woman are about, the value of life, balancing it out by the way you live, by the way you express it, not just in words but by living the sign that you believe — that you believe in man and woman. This is the heart of what I think I learned in Roscrea.)

Now my skills at Roscrea were still bad, terribly bad. I practically had to start from the beginning. The big problem was passing the state exams of Ireland. I wasn't yet studying to be a priest for any particular diocese or bishop. Roscrea was a place to get the necessary requirements. I still didn't learn much Gaelic. It was like one continuous class. There was recreation but most of the time was spent on Irish culture and Gaelic. We learned Irish dancing, too, and there were girls around, and it was a great lot of fun.

In the summer of 1960 I went to work in London. The Legion of Mary was sending volunteers to save the Irish emigrants who were losing their souls in England, especially the young people. This was my first experience of preaching — saying the rosary in Hyde Park at nine o'clock in the evening when it was still light outside, kneeling down on

40

the pavement and then getting up and talking about the Catholic faith. The people looked at us with amazement, as though we were crazy. I was eighteen. During the day I was working in Lyon's Cafe — for the whole summer.

It's incredible that my family allowed me to go. I was breaking all those ties that usually weren't broken. My father never left Ireland and he didn't think anyone else should. But I was the guy that was going to be a priest and they tolerated a lot of things for me because of that. It was really a tremendous adventure. I loved that summer — I enjoyed it a great deal. And believe it or not, by the end of that summer there were a lot of people who began taking instructions in the Catholic faith. Also I made some beautiful friends.

In London we lived in a big apartment building, the Legion of Mary headquarters. One could compare us to Vista Volunteers in this country only our purpose was the saving of souls. One of the groups opened up a kind of half-way house for prostitutes, for young Irish girls who had come over from Ireland and had gone astray. These girls were becoming a real social issue. When they came from Ireland they were very warm people, but very naive, and there were hustlers waiting at the station for them in London. We tried helping these young people by getting them different jobs. Of course, the Legion of Mary in this country is not that kind of thing. I'm hoping the Legion of Mary has become more political but I'm not sure that it has. The main emphasis was on the faith, and sometimes that didn't seem to be relevant at all. But there were good aspects. We were young but we began to see that there were issues and eventually this would lead into some sort of social concern. That played a big part in my life.

I came home at the end of August because I had a chance to go to the Eucharistic Congress in Munich. Some people, friends I had met in London, were going and asked me if I wanted to go. Now, I didn't have much money and I didn't have any way to go there, but they were going to get me a ticket for nothing. But I wanted to go back to Ireland first and it took a whole two days traveling by train and boat. Those boat trips were something else. The culture of the Irish, the praying of the rosary on the boat and singing of songs and sleeping on the decks — great experiences in my youth. My education was a street education in a sense, as the kids today would classify it. It was experimental. I wasn't afraid to hustle my way and I was always on my own.

I came back home and my mother met me. I remember it was a Monday morning when I got off the boat and she was so happy to see me because she hadn't seen me for the two and a half months I had been working in London. We had just finished embracing and I said, "Well, Mom, I'm leaving again on Thursday. I'm going to Europe." She thought I was crazy, that I was out of my mind. She really thought it was just a silly idea of the moment and that I'd go home and settle down.

Well, when Thursday morning came I went to my father and he was happy to see me back so I could get some work done. I told him, "Well, daddy, I'm leaving for Europe today. Could you give me twelve pounds?" And of course, my father could curse a lion out of heaven. He said, "I've had piles of work for you here and you go back to school and you haven't learned a damn thing this summer. And damma," — he used to say "damma" — "now you want to leave again!" He finally gave me twelve pounds and I went. I never knew why he gave it to me. I never understood it. So I thanked them, and I was on the bus on my way to Dublin and off to the boat.

I had never been to Europe before. I went back to London first to meet my friends and then we took a boat from Dover to Belgium and then a train to Munich. I spent almost two weeks there and experienced so much. The thing that struck me so much about the Eucharistic Congress was all those bishops and cardinals. I was simply overwhelmed. I had never met a cardinal in my life. I just had to shake hands with a cardinal. Hell, I went wild and shook hands with eleven of them. I even met an African cardinal, this tall black guy from southern Africa, one of the first black cardinals. Suddenly the real picture of the universality of the Church became so real to me. I met this young priest with whom I had worked in London who was of the Byzantine rite. He was being consecrated a bishop and he invited me to his consecration. I had a special invitation and for me that was really incredible. There I experienced a whole new part of the Church that I never knew before. For example, I received the Eucharist under both species, bread and wine, something lay people could not do in the Roman rite at that time. The bishop's consecration was three hours long, a whole new cultural thing for me, a real education.

I was on my own when I got into Munich and I couldn't speak any German. But I was always the kind of guy who could lead people around even though I didn't know what the hell it was all about. So, I was asked to be a guide — in Munich. I'd been there two days! But I'd been all over town. I couldn't speak German but I was always asking people directions and had no problem getting around town. So I was a guide for about twenty-five English-speaking tourists. I got to know this one family and they gave me their home to use. They got me tickets to do everything, and it didn't cost me a cent to get anywhere I wanted to go. I went to all the special lectures and to all the other activities of the Congress.

Cardinal Suenens of Belgium was a key figure there. He was involved in the Legion of Mary and I was very deep into the Legion of Mary

42

as a lay apostle. I was very interested in the whole lay apostolate thing, and already saw the real possibilities, the reality of the Church in terms of the lay apostolate. I never could understand why the hierarchy always would limit us. "Well," they'd say, "you're just lay people and you can just do certain things for the Church." I always felt so much a part of the Church, that I was as much a part of the Church as the pope or the bishop, except that they had special jobs.

Anyway, I got to speak with Suenens. He gave a fantastic lecture at that time emphasizing the laity and their role in the Church. It was in four languages and that overwhelmed me too — again the universality idea. It really convinced me that the Church was my world. In addition the Eucharistic Congress had brought so much emphasis on culture.

For example, I was so impressed with the African Church. I really saw black people for the first time although I had known blacks in London. There, most of them were poor. I used to work with some at Lyons Cafe and they were treated like dirt. They did the same menial tasks as you would expect the blacks to be doing in this country. But at the Congress I saw the cultural part of the blacks, and the African culture. This was the first time we heard the "Missa Luba," the African Mass set to drums. Fantastic!

Among other things, the European experience taught me never to be afraid. Even if I didn't know the language, that wasn't a hindrance to me at all. I had this drive to be open and to be searching. This operated very early in my youth. I always refused to say that I was a dumb kid. Some people would tell me, "You're dumb — you can't learn your books well." But my schooling was so bad in my youth that I always knew it was the school that was dumb.

Early in life, then, I became a determined man. My father and the village people told me when I was fifteen and came home from the Brothers, "Ah, you gave up too easily. You gave up. You're a failure. You're becoming a failure." I was so determined that I said they'd never tell me that I'm a failure. Like today I'm saying to Nixon and Johnson, bars aren't going to stop anyone's manhood. So there's always been this drive. The same was true when I left the seminary in this country, convinced that the Church was not speaking to the questions that were tearing men's lives apart. I am convinced that a layman can rehabilitate the Church.

After my experience in Munich, I had a lot of things happen to me. I got to see much of Germany. I walked with a group of people from Munich to Dachau. It brought the whole second world war picture before me and I began to understand what Dachau was about — the smell of the ovens — you could still smell something of the bodies of some million Jews that had died in Dachau. The horror of it!

43

I stayed with a German family in the parish there. The father had been involved in the second world war and he used to cry when the war was discussed. He couldn't speak any English at all, but the daughter could. The father kept asking for forgiveness for Germany, and did everything to make me feel at home. The German people in Munich couldn't give us enough welcome. I think that's why Pius XII really wanted the Eucharistic Congress in Munich that year. He saw the need to heal a lot of the wounds that Germany had certainly inherited as a result of the second world war. People there really went out of their way and the thing that came across was the need for forgiveness, for us to forgive them. For me the war had been rather abstract, but I then began to really understand much more deeply what it was all about, the history and the horror of that war and of every war.

Then, being in the south of Germany, I got this chance to go to Oberammergau and I went to the Passion Play. What an education! That whole vast month was just fantastic. Then I got another bus (I never had a damn cent in my pocket) and went to the Eagle's Nest, where Hitler was raised and that whole picture became very visible and very real. The beauty of that village and the beauty of that area is unbelievable.

Then I went to Austria and Salzburg and experienced some of the culture of that country before I finally got back to England and to Ireland. When I got back to Ireland, I immediately went back to Roscrea to school for the year.

(In 1960, a man by the name of Father McGraw, an Irish priest, a native of the County Tipperary, visited Roscrea from the diocese of Pueblo, Colorado. An emigrant from Ireland, he had gone to the United States, to the diocese of Pueblo, and had worked there for many years as a priest. He was now looking for vocations, what we call vocations, for young men to be priests in the U.S., in the name of Bishop Buswell, the bishop of the Pueblo diocese. A diocese is an area of a country governed by a bishop and the bishop is responsible for the spiritual life of the people, all the people. Many U.S. dioceses sent priests to Ireland to recruit, especially dioceses in the South where there has been a shortage of priests. Some of these Irish priests have problems here. Sometimes something goes wrong when they get here. Some get caught up with materialism and forget their faith and become quite domineering like some of the Irish priests in Ireland. Most of these Irish priests in the U.S. were educated in Ireland and brought out after they were ordained.

Bishop Buswell, however, is what we call a pastoral bishop. He is one of the bishops consecrated by Pope John XXIII. A pastoral bishop, to my mind, is a bishop without the fancy training that many bishops get. Most bishops are trained in the colleges of Rome, related to the Roman Church. Many of them have a Doctor of Divinity degree. Many of them have spent most of their time in executive positions in the Church, like in the chancery offices of the dioceses.

But Bishop Buswell was a parish priest, a man of the people, before being a bishop, plus the fact that he is a very extraordinary, very warm person. John XXIII was a similar kind of man and probably that's what made Pope John the most extraordinary man of our own times — that he was a warm man, that he knew people, he knew people's problems, he knew their frailties. An executive tends to be far removed from his people and doesn't have that sensitivity because he is dealing with books and papers, a kind of business manager who never gets down to touching human life and touching the sorrow and pain and anxiety of living.

But Buswell is one of Pope John's bishops who was more pastoral than executive. Because Bishop Buswell is interested in pastoral work, he wanted the people who were going to be priests in his diocese to know the people there. He wasn't just going to bring an Irish priest over and fill the ranks because he needed a priest to say Mass. He wanted a priest that knew the culture of this country, knew the society, and as early as possible, particularly during the seminary years. I was one of those people.)

In July of 1961, I received a letter from Bishop Buswell in Pueblo saying that he had decided that I should prepare for the priesthood in the States. Without question, immediately I prepared to leave for America.

I realized now that everything I was, everything I had done — my experiences in traveling, my very individualistic ways — had prepared me for this rigorous, most difficult task — leaving everything. My mother, my father, my family, brothers and sisters, all the culture, everything that I knew, and on my own, I was leaving it all — and beginning a whole new way of life in a new land, a land that I had only just read about.

During my experiences in Roscrea I used to read *Time* magazine and a lot of books on my own, too, though my reading ability was always very limited and very bad because of my earlier education. But I always managed it even though I was slow, and I didn't have the fast skills of learning. I was very inquisitive, and I read the kinds of things I felt were necessary. I always kept up on politics and then after the Munich experience, I was very much into the Church, especially when there was talk about a Vatican Council. I remember the election of Pope John. Two hundred of us were waiting under loudspeakers out in the yard in Roscrea. Who was Pope John? Who was this old man? And then the whole idea of Vatican Council — the most discussed event for years — the first council in a hundred years. What would this all mean?

It certainly meant that I began to have new ideas about the Church. The idea of being a priest began to be more real to me. So when Bishop

Buswell decided to bring me to the States, I immediately went to the embassy and started filling out papers for emigration.

I remember the day I got the letter. I was making hay in Ireland, and I always say that I could still be making hay in Ireland if it wasn't for this mystery that I don't even understand. I said yes, I'm going, no hesitation, that's where I want to go, that's where I have to be.

Of course, the whole thing really overwhelmed my parents. It was very hard on my father. For the first time in my life we were beginning to talk together and I could see he was really a very beautiful man. In spite of or because of this hard work that he had done all his life, he was really a beautiful man. I felt very, very close to my father at this time.

But my parents did not object. This was part of the Irish mentality — God's will is God's will. You accept it and you go on and that's the task. That was part of our history, our heritage. Irish history is full of missionaries who took Christ literally and left everything to follow Him.

We planned the trip by boat to New York and we started looking up any relatives we had in America. We had three cousins who were nuns on my mother's side down in New Orleans. My mother also had a cousin in New York and we wrote to her and she's the one who met me at the boat. There were all kinds of other cousins who had gone to America, some of them already passed away. All Irish people have a lot of ties with America.

So we prepared and within six weeks, I was all set. I didn't want anyone to come to the boat except my brother Dan and a friend of his, a young German who was studying for the priesthood and was staying with us for the summer. We had to drive down to Cobh in County Cork which was almost 250 miles away from my home. We drove down the day before and stayed in Cork that night and went to a dance. I remember going out in the boat to the ship which couldn't come into Cobh Harbor because it was too big.

(It is significant that I decided to come by boat. I could have come by plane, but that only takes a few hours. I came by boat, which takes five days, because I knew I just couldn't land in a culture that was totally different than what I was born into, a people who were different than I, with value systems different than I, and I wanted to break into that culture slowly.)

It was only then when I got on the ship that I realized the departing — and God it was incredible — that part of dying is really incredible. Everything that I knew and loved and I would never come back. America was another world. It was totally different from England or Europe. Culturally it would be totally different. And it was so far across the Atlantic. In Ireland, to go twenty-five miles was something else, but now to go over 3,000 miles by boat, alone, and I knew it was about half way when

I made it to New York. That was hard to conceive at that time. How many emigrants from Ireland must have felt that way!

The last thing I remember seeing was the St. Patrick Cathedral on the hill in Cobh and the green hills of Ireland. I prayed the prayer of St. Patrick that any man who left that shore someday would return with a blessing. And so I hoped I would come back to my people, but I was going and I was happy to leave, even though there were the tears and the sad waving of the handkerchiefs.

The beautiful part was that I wasn't lonely. I may have been lonely for a while — no I really wasn't ever lonely. I was so sure of what I was about. I had to do what I was doing even though it was sad, very sad to leave my family. My work was important, where I was going was important and I wanted to go even though the parting was like tearing apart my whole life.

CHAPTER THREE

Getting to New York was so exciting, mainly because I always thought of America as the hospitality house of the world for so many people for so long, rescuing people from oppression, many of them my own people. I couldn't wait to see the Statue of Liberty, that welcoming sign of a free people.

(In fact, you had a sense of what it was for the immigrants who came to this country in the 1800's when they saw that great lamp which they knew in Ireland and all of Europe, the lamp of freedom, the Statue of Liberty.)

I remember we got up quite early in the morning and could feel the heat and the smell of New York coming across the bay. We all were out on deck, including the Americans, many of whom had been away for some time from their native land, and they wanted to smell America and feel America again because it meant something to them.)

I couldn't believe the hot air coming out of New York. We were still about a hundred miles off shore and there was this breeze of hot air — this new climate that I had never been in before — this terrible hot air, sweltering in about the middle of August, and humid as hell.

Arriving in New York was a great thrill. I was just overwhelmed by the size of things. And the city! It was marvelous — such excitement!

(I think the big thing that struck me when we pulled into New York harbor was the big yellow cabs. I had never seen anything like this in my life. They were incredible. The size of them and the color of them. I had never seen yellow cars before.

I was quite overwhelmed by the material, by the quantity of goods. For example, when I went to a supermarket I couldn't believe it. Of course, I'd never seen a supermarket before. There was so much of everything — just everything and anything was available. In Ireland, we used to eat turkey once a year. But here people could have turkey every day.

I had idealized the freedom in the United States as most Irish and as most immigrants do. It's not easy to see the subtlety of racism here and I didn't know about the real poverty that was here. That came later.

(Some relatives from my mother's side met me, some of whom had been here for years. I stayed in New York three days. I'll never forget it. The heat almost killed me. It was stifling and almost like you couldn't breathe. I understand now as we move into ecology, that much of this was and is due to pollution.

From New York I flew to Denver, United Airlines, my very first flight. Landing in Denver was a whole new experience because of the mountains. I was overwhelmed by America and its magnificence — the stretch of the land and the snow-capped mountains. I had never seen such grandeur before.

I was headed for St. Thomas Seminary in Denver, but I knew I was a few days early and the seminary would not be open. I didn't have anybody to meet me, and I didn't know where I was going to stay, but I met a young boy on the plane going out, a young boy about thirteen years of age who was sitting beside me. He was coming back from visiting an aunt in New York City. I told him who I was, and that I was coming from Ireland and that I didn't know where I was going when I would get to Denver. Without hesitation or doubt he told me his father and mother were picking him up and that he was sure they would take me to his home.

Well, they did take me home. The young man's father was a psychologist for the United States Army, and he was stationed at the army base in Denver, Colorado. I stayed with them the first three days in Denver before I went to St. Thomas Seminary. They have remained my friends ever since that time. The father has since left the army and now is doing private practice in California. When I told him about what happened about the action of the Milwaukee 14, I didn't hear from him for a long time. But recently I heard from them, and they wrote that their youngest son, the one who was on the plane with me, was subject to be drafted. He was about the ninety-first on the list and they were wondering what I could do, if I could give them any help, any advice. I think it's an extraordinary state of affairs, that here is a man who was in high command, a colonel in the army, now in private practice, who finds himself facing the fears of the young — the same fears that the poor of this country have always feared when their sons went off to war. What an extraordinary change of affairs.)

Anyway, I stayed with these wonderful people and I got to know the whole army scene pretty well. Later they moved to Ft. Carson. During the first six months of my seminary training, I used to visit them there. From that military base, I got some idea of the size and the monstrous proportions and scope of the military. The colonel brought me to the town the military was building under Pike's Peak in Colorado Springs. I was amazed, but I never really put it together until recently. The whole concept of how the military and being a soldier related to my Christianity hadn't been worked out at all yet.

(But, you know, in early Christianity, a Christian soldier could never kill. Men could be soldiers, perhaps, and be baptized in the Christian community. But some of the Fathers of the Church said it was better to turn away a soldier than have him remain a soldier and be a Christian. We got away from this heritage about the third century, when Constantine was the emperor of Rome, and the Church was accepted, the Christian community of the Church of Jesus was accepted as the state religion of that empire. Of course, later, the empire, the state, tried to make Christians out of everybody, often at the point of a sword — which is totally contradictory to the message of Jesus.

Jesus's message was one of invitation. He always said: "Come follow me, be my friends, my people, come and be my men and women." He never told people they *had* to be "my men" — be His men and women. He always said: "Come. Come follow me!" Of course, Constantine said "You'd better be His men or else." The whole message of Jesus got very corrupted from that time on. It is only through rare individuals who crossed pages of history since that time that we have examples of Christians. It's no wonder that G. K. Chesterson said: "It's not that Christianity has failed. It's been found hard and so found untried."

And, of course, I say the same thing about non-violence. Non-violence has not failed. It's been found hard and so found untried.

I feel that Christianity has not had a golden age — except perhaps in certain countries. We had a golden age in Ireland for the first six or seven centuries of Irish history. The Irish had the monasteries. Ireland was the island of saints and scholars. In a sense, the Irish were a scholastic people. They were people who were educated, who felt the dignity of life.

There are many other groups of Christians throughout Europe and the world who were extraordinary groups of people who kept the lamp of freedom alive. They took no part in killing and murder. Today you find the Christian message mostly on the side of murder, murder as another word for war. It's a word we don't like to hear, but it's a reality, brothers and sisters. It's a reality. People are killed on both sides. The Vietnamese kill us. We kill the Vietnamese. There's murder on both sides. You can't say it's not, you see. People try to describe what's happening in different words: the Vietnamese are protecting their land: the Americans are said to be exploiting. But you see, the murder is a very real thing; and that's, of course, the hardest thing to tell men because that's when you stand alone on both sides.

I think I became more and more convinced as I passed through a period of four years of looking for answers, working for answers, trying to understand what sensitivity is, knowing how inadequate we are as persons in ourselves and in our own lives to meet human needs and meet one another as persons, that it becomes harder to say what we know the truth is. But the truth has to be spoken because the truth is the only thing that means anything in the end of history and at the end of time. We are helping to bring about what we call the omega point of history, what Jesus called the Kingdom of God, what the young people are calling the Age of Aquarius. We're trying to bring about that time — that time when men and women can be more human, where war will not be a part of their lives, where war will not be a word that would be spoken or lived or seen.

Are we mad to dream these dreams? I would say no. I know nothing else to work for that's worth dreaming because certainly division among men and women is no way to the future. Today, war — the war in Vietnam is certainly causing the rotting of our cities. And I'll get into a little bit of that because it became a part of my life. It's a part of why I burned files. It's a part of why I became involved in a hospitality house. The victims of the Vietnam war — Bud, Herbert and Patsy — the skid row men who testified at my trial in my behalf, these are the victims of Vietnam. These are the people who are dispossessed as a result of that war, mainly because of priorities.

I think you can change those priorities and I can change them. The judge can change and the jury and the defense and prosecution can change them. But we're faced with a tremendous responsibility, a tremendous amount of uncertainty. We're not quite sure if these dreams could be real. Our sense of values, our very senses have been numbed by the threat of materialism. Our sense of values has been numbed as a result of the misuse of the communication media.

The media today are very seldom used to bring the message of truth to us. In fact, when the media do show problems of hunger and housing, people in high command are outraged. But the truth is there to see. Malnutrition is a word and a reality in the United States and something we have to face. The rotting of our cities is a reality in our United States and not a false truth, and it has to be met by all of us. And when the media bring that truth to us, we must welcome it and celebrate.

But the media today are used to sell things, products. And so, at night on the news, a man makes a statement about the burning of a house or some very terrible anxiety, something very anxious that was happening, and all of a sudden, there's a man selling cars, just like that! My God! You just don't do those things! People must hear the news. If you want to sell things, put them all at the end of the news or at the beginning. We must use the media to make our lives much fuller. We must use technology not to develop bombs and guns and death instruments and napalm and defoliants, but to make our lives more whole.

These are things I came to understand. These are the reasons I am here — because I know I must speak. I don't speak with malice. I don't speak with anger in the sense that I hold anyone of you responsible for where we are. We're all responsible. I'm responsible. You're responsible. And we can change it if we change it together, you see.

It is interesting that the first friends I made in America were a military family. After a couple of days with them I took a bus down to Pueblo because I had to see Pueblo. The bishop wasn't in town at the time, but I did meet some of the priests from the diocese of Pueblo.

The city of Pueblo is not a very rich part of Colorado. It's rich in the sense that it's industrial, but it's one of the less beautiful cities in Colorado. Colorado is such an extraordinary state, such a beautiful state, but Pueblo doesn't have all that beauty. It's a steel town that seemed to have a lot of poverty when I was there. It had the usual two sides of the tracks, one side a little richer than the other. But I didn't spend too much time there.

In fact, during my seminary years, it was mostly study. I studied the first year at St. Thomas Seminary in Denver.)

The first vacation I had at St. Thomas was at Christmas and I didn't want to stick around Denver. I finally decided I'd take off for New York and down to Delaware to visit a friend-schoolmate of my mother's. So, in my first four months here I had crossed the country again, by train this time. It was there in Delaware that I drank my first glass of beer. I hadn't had a drink (alcoholic, that is) since I was ten when I got confirmed and took the pledge. I was supposed to wait until I was twenty-one but I was just twenty.

I came back to St. Thomas and finished out the year. But just as in Roscrea, Latin was a real problem and at that time yet, Latin was considered essential to become a priest. So it was decided that I would take Latin during the summer at Conception Abbey, the Benedictine school outside of St. Joseph, Missouri.

So I spent a summer there and that was a great experience — a great learning experience — although I must confess that I didn't learn much Latin. But I experienced the great Benedictine spirit and especially their liturgy.

The thing that really made the summer exciting was the Vatican Council. The Council was at its most mind-blowing time, Conception Abbey had invited the Redemptorist, Father Bernard Haering, an expert at the Council, to lecture there. It is impossible to describe the spirit, the hope, the enthusiasm that we all shared. The Church was our life, and the Church was being born again. She was putting on a whole new dress, and instead of being a cold, plain stone statue, tucked away in an empty niche where no one could see her, she was stepping out into society, fresh and alive — and human. We were breathless looking at her again (perhaps for the first time) and asking her questions again (perhaps for the first time.)

That fall I moved again — this time to Mount Calvary, Wisconsin, a college seminary run by the Capuchin Fathers. Bishop Buswell felt that I had some more catching up to do, and he felt that this would be a good place for me to do it. So again I changed scenes and experienced the thought and life of another religious community, as well as another locale and culture in the American scene. The educational value of this is hard to overestimate.

(So, it was in the fall of 1962, that I began studying at St. Lawrence Seminary, Mount Calvary, Wisconsin, which is outside Fond du Lac, and that's where a lot of things began happening to my life. Again I felt that our studies at Mount Calvary were boring and unrelated to the real world. But I have very precious memories of the friendships I made there and of the silence and of some of the studies that I really got into.

One of them was history. I hadn't been much of a student of history before that time. In fact, I read more Irish history in those two years at Calvary than I ever had in Ireland. I began to read my own history because it became important. James Joyce said you have to leave Ireland to come to respect it and like it. Shaw said the same thing. I guess it's very true.

Then I got into American history, which I had never studied before, and I found people like Tom Jefferson and the fathers of this country having very real parallels to people with whom I identify in my heritage — people like St. Patrick, you know, or people in the Irish centers of study, or Irish adventurers, guys going out to start a new life. The fathers of this country came here to begin a new life and create a new land.

I began to study Church history which was also new for me, on a global scale, not just Irish Catholic history, but history that involved the community of faith, which involves the Jewish community, and the Catholic community, and the Protestant community. I was especially interested in the Reformation period, and what that meant at that time. People like Martin Luther became real for me for the first time. I opened my eyes to the corruption of the Church of Luther's time and I could

53

visualize him nailing his ninety-five theses to the church door, making demands of the Church.

What struck me the hardest was that these men of history were not extraordinary people. I know there's been certain references to saints and Christ and all like that here to me during this trial, which is kind of a — kind of not just shocking but overwhelming. I believe that unless we compare ourselves to ordinary men, nothing gets done in history.

We must look at people like Thomas More, a man of the law, a man who had his head removed as a result of an act of conscience, or people like St. Thomas Aquinas and his struggle for truth, not as extraordinary men. Men gifted with ability, yes, and who used that ability. I see men like Thomas Jefferson, not as an extraordinary man, but a man who had a sense for people and a sense for freedom and a man who was brave enough to risk his entire future for the possibility of making a dream. People like Martin King, not an extraordinary man, though we would like to make him extraordinary because then we never relate to him. People like Gandhi. If Gandhi was different from your flesh and mine, then we have no part of him. In the same way, if Christ were different from your flesh and mine, we have very little to relate to, because it is men and women, people we can touch and feel, who are part of our bones and the structure and the history of the planet, to whom and with whom we can relate. Only real men and women, people like ourselves, have made and shaped history.

In our times I see people like the Father Berrigans and the Father Groppis as real people who are making history, who are shaping destiny. I am sure Jefferson confronted the people of his time and I can look back at the Irish Rebellion and see people like Pat Pierce, who confronted the people of his time and everyone thought he was crazy — until after he was shot — then they said he was a hero. And many people thought King was a mad man, a lot of people in Chicago, for example. When he went down into a white section of the city, the people threw rocks and bottles at him. Now he's a hero. Mayor Daley named a street after King, because now he's safe — he's dead!

You see, Jefferson I am sure was the same kind of man. Jefferson was a guy who interrupted the status quo. He wasn't merely interested in the taxes being taken from this country. He saw the possibilities of becoming a free people in a free land.

I have crossed this nation more than most Americans. I have spoken in thirty-five states. I feel that I must take my place at the side of people like Jefferson, not at all saying that I am as good or as great as he, but that I must try to be as good as he. We must try to be as good as people like Martin Luther who said, with all odds against him, "Here I stand, so God help me."

So there I stood in a triangle of Milwaukee with all of the city's rage and outrage coming on my head. And there I stood in jail with $30,000 bail on my head and away from my family. And here I stand with no future for myself and for my children, at least not for the next four or five years or maybe never. And here I begin a fight, hopefully a non-violent one, to bring about a change. And here I stand, so God help me!

Again, I think people like Jefferson were that kind of people when they decided to write the Declaration of Independence and the Constitution of the United States. They knew England had mighty armies and the colonies were ill-equipped, but they had to move on if they were going to bring the country and republic into being.

So the reading of history in those three years at Mount Calvary was important to me and the times were extraordinary, too.

For example, there were two important landmarks outside of the reading and studies and thinking I was doing as a seminarian preparing for the Roman Catholic priesthood

One, of course, was the Vatican Council that was going on in Rome in the '60's. Called by John XXIII, it was the most extraordinary thing that took place in the community of the Roman Catholic Church in centuries, and certainly has influenced the direction of where that Church is going to go in the next decades. Pope John himself was an embracing man. He was a man who knew people. He was a man who could cross out all the demarcation lines which had kept people apart and particularly on religious grounds — Jews against Catholics, Catholics against Jews, Catholics against Protestants and all the Protestant sects against one another.

John was saying it's a time for men to unite most deeply on these grounds, and for this reason he called an Ecumenical Council, a council that would try to embrace all faith communities, that would extend even to the Eastern World. People like Thomas Merton, for example, went to the East, trying to understand Eastern non-Christian monasticism. That's the rich part of our times. We are going to experience a great link between the East and the West. We have to be able to understand the Chinese people, for example, and the South Vietnamese. We are going to have to see ourselves as brothers and sisters of a common family, yellow brothers touching white brothers.

John embraced everyone and everyone knew it. In a deeply spiritual sense, John's warmth was so powerful because it went far beyond the man. We don't know how to explain it except we know it was there. We all felt John's influence, regardless of how divided the Church was on the global scale, even in the Catholic community. Even here in the United States we have some 40,000,000 Catholics. The Catholic Church owns about $80,000,000,000 worth of property in this country and we are a very powerful force, but we agree on very few things, except perhaps

55

in the essence of our faith. And as the Church in its old form breaks up, people are having a very hard time staying with it. The priests and nuns are leaving, and many lay people because the Mass isn't the way it was when it was in Latin and it was unrelated to the world and they didn't have to find meaning.

But there's no magic attached to the Church. It's related to real life, the life that people must live. We must be willing to enter and face the world as the early Christians did. We may have to enter the prisons and the lions' dens in order to prevail, in order for good men and good women to have a future.

This is what I found myself learning and becoming aware of. Vatican Council freed my mind. You see, the Church, the faith is a difficult thing to talk about, because it's not just something you learn. It's something you feel in the very depths of your bones, and if you really understand your faith, you live it. You are compelled, as we were compelled in essence, to act out that faith, whether it was by fasting, whether it was burning files, whether it's living the way I have been living the last year. That to me is something that comes out of your faith — being and everything that is in you that is human. These actions don't just come from the air. The faith permeates from above. It's something you feel and you act on and that's that.

So I found the Vatican Council opening up my mind and I began to reckon with the priesthood in these new terms, the priesthood as we have known it to be, in the form of clericalism. Clericalism means priests with all the garments, the externals, the privileges; professional religious men, often unrelated to our communities, who were supposedly able to give us the counsel that we need as lay people on spiritual problems, on problems that were troubling us, on marital problems, whatever they may be. So often these men were unreal, unreal.

Perhaps much of this is because seminary life was unreal. It had nothing to do with the real world. In most instances, it was isolated, and I felt that if the Vatican Council was going to move in the direction of John the XXIII, we had to get out of the seminary and find ourselves and find the world that we were going to be part of. And that's what I did in 1964.

There was also another thing happening in that time. Martin Luther King and his work in the South was a real confrontation in my life. Martin King confronted any person, particularly a white man, about the fact of being white and being privileged. Blacks were slaves who had come in the bottoms of slave ships, in chains, who had become our servants for centuries — for two, three centuries. And now, at this late hour in history, blacks are not free to travel and live and work and enter into the institution that this society was blessed with and privileged with. I found myself as a white immigrant, not even born here, though my mother was born here, having the privileges of being able to do many things that some of these black brothers and sisters were not allowed to do. King confronted me with that. And I said I couldn't accept the privilege of being a white man until my black brothers and sisters had some of those same privileges. And so I became very familiar with the black struggle, or the civil rights movements of the 1960's.)

So at Mount Calvary I was getting my head into all kinds of things. I was deep in the Church thing, reading all the contemporary Catholic magazines. I was enthusiastic about the new changes that were coming into the liturgy, and I was reading *Worship* magazine regularly. Although I was still studying for the priesthood, the theology of the lay priesthood appealed to me greatly — the realization that there would never be enough priests and nuns to do the job, that lay people, too, were members and part of the Church, and that this sleeping giant of the laity, as Pope Pius XII had already called the lay apostolate, was capable of immense good.

At St. Lawrence Seminary I was really a part of a small group who discussed these things very seriously while many other seminarians were either discussing or listening to or watching the Green Bay Packers. I had gathered a little library of my own and was doing a lot of reading. St. Lawrence gave me a bit of confidence in myself in the two years there. I learned to go ahead on my own, to think on my own, to have opinions about things that were not looked upon with a great deal of favor by the seminary officials who were generally very conservative.

But my years there again emphasized the need for prayer. I would get up early in the morning and walk outside, alone, in the freshness of the morning to pray and meditate. I learned how to be alone, how to be quiet. I have often longed for that kind of quiet after I left the seminary, and I think it's so necessary in the jumbled-up world today, in our fast-moving times, when there is very little time to stand still, and very little order in most people's lives, especially in the lives of the young. The value of the Mount Calvary years, and, of course, of my roots in Ireland came home to me most vividly the first time I went to jail. Because of that background, I had tremendous resources to draw from, I was able to use my time. Strange as it may sound, the seminary prepared me for jail.

Really, I think any of the fellows in jail will tell you that the priests are much more prepared for jail than most people are. Bob Gilliam, one of my best friends at Mount Calvary who later served two years at Sandstone Federal Penitentiary in Minnesota for draft resistance, told me he was most grateful for his year in the seminary. The seminary, he said, slowed him down and put him in some kind of order. You have to tolerate the order and yet remain in control of yourself. It was Gilliam, by the way, an absolute genius, with whom I used to rap about the Catholic Worker movement of Dorothy Day. Immediately after he left the seminary he joined the Catholic Worker staff in New York, and his enthusiasm had much to do with my starting Casa Maria, a Catholic Worker House in Milwaukee.

It's a strange kind of thing to talk about when you stand for freedom, but the experience of Mount Calvary taught me discipline and how to use my time. We weren't allowed to go galavanting around the neighborhood, wasting our time. We were not free to get out, and I didn't have any relatives to come visit me at the times the seminarians were permitted to have visitors. Many of the guys were stuck with relatives while I was in my room reading. I didn't like TV, and hell, I wasn't going to sit around moping. Even though many of the studies were boring, I read on my own because I realized I had to catch up to a lot of the things the other guys already had. So I kept my nose to the grindstone, and though my grades were bad to begin with, they began to pick up by the time I graduated in 1964 with some kind of associate arts degree.

Most important, I suppose, I became starved for knowledge and knew now that I had a mind capable of grasping profound subjects. This new confidence is most important to understand. I hope I have a chance to keep on studying, perhaps not in a formal way, but to do research, especially on the Church as we move into new times. I keep saying the Church because that's the most important thing to me; the Church as a sign to God, a sign of life. We are all responsible for that sign, to make that sign visible. I would like to do more studying on mysticism and monastic life and communities and do some experimenting along these lines, acting out the history of the Church. I want to really be able to read Scripture. From the Scriptures and from the history of the Church, can we look at our times and create new communities? These things have to be discussed and tried.

In my final year at St. Lawrence the civil rights thing became more and more real to me. It was really the discrimination against black people that opened my eyes to the injustices surrounding me in this country.

It was this discrimination that made me begin to see the problems of the poor, and I began to ask where the Church was in all these matters. I began to see the inadequacies of the priesthood. The priesthood was evidently not speaking to some. Why was the priesthood so silent in the face of racism? Why were the bishops in Mississippi going along with racist policies — just as they have gone along with the war questions?

It became more and more clear to me that the reason the Church was not doing anything was that the Church had become secure. The priesthood would provide a way to security. To be a real priest you would have to be a daring priest, a rabble-rousing priest, ostracized by the rest of the Church, even its clergy and hierarchy.

And then the whole celibacy thing began to hit me. I realized that celibacy could not be imposed on anybody. Celibacy had to be invitational, and if it wasn't, the Church was not the Church of invitation but the Church of coercion — which is the same as the state. And to me, that's when the Church becomes a false god. As an institution, it becomes a false prophet. The Church has to be able to invite men to life, and that's the only reason it's a sign of life, that's the only time it has the fact of love operating. The Church can invite only out of love. When the Church loses its sense of roots and its sense of love it has lost the whole concept of Christ — because I can only see Christ as love, as this man with a tremendous capacity to love, who invites people to do things — to follow Him, to give what you have to the poor. Christ is always invitational, never condemning.

The Church has to be invitational to people who want to serve. The Church as the sign, the sacrament of Christ, must be free to say to all men, "Come." And this invitation must not be in just one form. Celibacy is one form, but I knew then and I know now that there have to be married clergy.

And I began to see the absurdity of the divisions in the Church between bishops, priests and laity. Different offices by reason of different gifts, yes, but a priest should not be known by what he wears or where he lives, but by the fact that he is a leader and has a great love for his task, his work, his people. And the bishop should be recognizable by an even greater love he has for mankind, not by a special cross and rings and collar. I began to have this vision of the Church of the future.

Priests of the future must arise from the community and the people must want them to become their priests. The people must want them to lead them, and especially, to lead them in prayer. How absurd to ordain a man just because he has come through eight formal years of study and has passed all his examinations. Surely, we need scholars, but there can also be lay Church scholars. But the priest must truly be a leader, with the people, building a community of faith and love.

After my first year at Mount Calvary, I had the whole summer free and I wasn't sure what I was going to do. I thought of going back to Colorado to work in the diocese in some form, like in a parish or something. But I had met some friends from Wausau, Wisconsin, and it was because of them that I decided to spend the summer in Wisconsin. I had no close relatives near-by so I never was tied to going home anyplace, and I certainly wasn't going to go back to Ireland or anything like that.

So I went to Wausau to work at the hospital and to earn a little money. But during that summer I was always into something. **One of** the first things I did was organize a youth program in Wausau. The young people had nowhere to go during the summer except to the bars. A few of the bars were pretty famous for roudy parties and the usual carryings-on of young college kids. It seemed to me that it was kind of a tragedy that a lot of young people had no place to talk about some of the serious things, as well as to enjoy themselves. So a young medical student and myself developed a kind of a social awareness discussion group that would involve itself in hootenannies in the out-of-doors and hikes up the mountains in the surrounding areas. By July we had a good group going — maybe as many as forty to fifty people. We had a retreat that summer, too, during which we used various tapes and talks and held open discussions about some of the issues. I had a tape of Dr. Tom Dooley, a man who was really interesting at the time. I know now that much of his feeling about Communism certainly has permeated the American foreign policy today in terms of Vietnam. But you can't get away from the fact that he was so human, that he was doing important work, that he was almost like Albert Schweitzer. It's just unfortunate that his understanding of Communism and of the whole plight of that part of Asia was rather blurred. Anyhow, we really did have some fine experiences.

It was at the end of that summer that I met Netty, the year before I left the seminary. I never thought of her as a girlfriend. In fact, I never planned that she would be any kind of deep, intimate friend. Sometimes I feel that women have a strange way of deciding when they see a man whom they want. They can really get what they want. I really feel I was trapped — although I welcomed the trap.

It was toward the end of the summer. I was ready to go back to the seminary. In the cafeteria one night, I was on the second shift and had gone down to dinner with a bunch of the young nurses. There's a nursing school there, too, and there were always a lot of the young nurses around — and young orderlies. A couple of them asked me what I was going to do that evening and I told them I usually walk in the evening. I used to walk quite a few miles through the town of Wausau, kind of a nice town, and the countryside was beautiful around there. Sometimes I'd climb the surrounding hills, alone, meditating. Anyway, someone said she would like to come along and I figured that all the kids there were going to come along. So I said OK, but that I had to get out of the white orderly clothes I was wearing. That meant I had to go to the place where I was staying. I had been staying at the home of an old German lady who sort of made her home my home. I was able to have my friends there and be very open with her. She was like a mother and she considered me her son — a very beautiful woman.

So, I went "home" to change my clothes and clean up. Well, who should show up in the car but one of the guys I knew and his girl —

and — Netty! They all arrived in the car. Wow! My seminary training, celibacy! My God! Single dates are dangerous for seminarians! So I had to re-adjust my Irish and seminary training. Well, anyhow, we walked that evening and we walked — and we talked.

But even then it never occurred to me what might happen. I guess the thing that attracted me most about Netty is that she was the daughter of a farmer. And she was a nurse. And she was very open. But I was thrilled about the idea of farming because I — because my father was a farmer and I had never been on an American farm — at least never on a Wisconsin farm — I had been on an Iowa farm. But her farm was only seventy miles away and she was finishing nursing school in about two weeks and. . .

Anyway, Netty asked me to come and visit their farm. I went there right before I returned to the seminary and was really taken in — mostly by the simplicity of her family, their lives, their hard work. I guess the truth is they reminded me very much of home. It wasn't their poverty. It was their simplicity. They accepted me — they did nothing special for me. They were just farmers — with a simple kind of faith operating in their lives. Netty's father is a convert to Catholicism. Her mother is a cradle Catholic but the faith meant basically that they were God-fearing people. They went to Mass on Sunday and they prayed at the meals. The faith was simply part of their lives.

I slept on the couch while I stayed there and I'm not sure how they felt about me. I was kind of overwhelmed by it all and I did get to know Netty better. I went to one of their local fairs, one of these Northern Wisconsin fairs with all the cattle coming in.

Nothing much came of the visit — except that I asked her to marry me. This was my third date with her. She thought I was crazy and I probably was.

But, I was determined to go back to the seminary because I felt that I really needed to put my life into some order and understand where I was really headed. I spent that next year in the seminary but in six months I was engaged. I must have been one of the first seminarians who was engaged while still in the seminary — six months before I left. I was advancing the Church's history. I'm sure it's happening almost every day now. At that time it was culturally shocking and it was a little hard to cope with it intellectually because it was against tradition. But to me it was the right thing to do. Netty came to visit me, of course. It was always very embarrassing when she would come to visit me because at that time seminarians got very embarrassed when girls came to visit them.

But Netty never made any bones about it. It never occurred to her that it was odd for a seminarian to have his girlfriend visit him in the seminary. She wrote to me quite often during that year, and one of the letters was caught by the priest who, believe it or not, had the authority to open our mail. He figured that this girl was writing to me too often and he opened my letter. I didn't get angry. I knew he had that authority. I had grown up in that tradition and it didn't particularly bother me. In some ways now it would be quite shocking.

Luckily, the priest who opened the letter was a man for whom I had the greatest respect and still have. Well, he brought me this letter and asked me about this girlfriend thing. He was rather good about it and we talked about it. I told him how I felt about her and that I probably would not continue after June. But I told him I wanted to finish out the year — if he would allow me — because it was important to me as a person. It was important to me to see how I was doing intellectually, how I was doing in my studies. Also, I was deep into what the faith was all about. Amazingly, he told me I could finish the year. I will always be most grateful. Had I left then I would not have simply missed graduation. I would have left not knowing — not knowing if I really had something upstairs to work with. I had to know — I had to get my head together on a lot of other things.

I came out of the seminary in June. Netty came to the graduation and again this was kind of embarrassing because intellectually I knew where I was, but emotionally I couldn't deal with it. Now, of course, it's all kind of foolish, but at that time it was very, very real.

At any rate, I left the seminary. But I want to stress how important Mount Calvary was in my life — stifling in some forms, but those were three important years. They were important because I wasn't immediately thrown into the American culture when I came here. The seminary prepared me gradually and I was able to be away from the culture, yet able to study within it.

When I came out, many problems confronted me. I really didn't know what I was going to do. I didn't have any of the human resources. I didn't have any relatives near-by. I didn't have any funds to go into graduate studies.

(Let's face it, when I left the seminary, I was ill-equipped to do much. I puttered around with odd jobs for a while. I wanted to go to medical school, but I didn't have sufficient money. So I found myself working in hospitals because I wanted to work on behalf of people whom I thought were in need.)

But, of course, Netty was on my mind. She had moved to Milwaukee and was going with another guy and she wasn't sure I was going to be her guy. So then I got determined that she was going to be my girl. No guy was going to beat me. I decided I would come to Milwaukee. If she had been in Denver I would have moved to Denver.

62

Before I left the seminary I had applied to work in a hospital in Milwaukee. I had a job waiting for me when I came out. I was planning to go to school at the University of Wisconsin-Milwaukee, but I applied at the Milwaukee Technical School because it wouldn't cost me as much money. But I was working full-time and after two or three months I found that I just didn't have enough time. Besides, I was getting tired and the education was not interesting me. It was more important to get myself together.

Just three months after I left the seminary Netty and I contracted a formal engagement. I saved all my money and bought this emerald ring because an emerald is a symbol of life and love and love breaks easy. A diamond lasts forever. An emerald won't. So I bought her a green emerald worth $500. I broke my back to get the money, got the emerald set, and the engagement was officially on.

It wasn't long before we decided to get married. Netty's sister, Catherine, was getting married the day after Christmas and so we decided to get married the same day and make it a double wedding even though we had intended to wait another year.

The double wedding was held in Rib Lake, Wisconsin, on December 26, 1964, and it was twenty below zero. Three priests concelebrated the nuptial Mass: Father Werner Hemmelgarn, C.PP.S., the pastor of Rib Lake, Father Charles Froelich, C.PP.S., of Westboro, Wisconsin, and Father Alexis Luzi, O.F.M. Cap., of St. Anthony's Monastery in Marathon City, a priest whom I had grown to like and respect when I was working in Wausau.

The Mass was truly beautiful. A group of my seminarian buddies provided the singing and they were great. The people of the town couldn't get over how beautiful everything was. Even the pastor the next day commented in his sermon on how beautiful the Mass and singing were at the wedding. He also said that he hoped not all the seminarians would end up like Mike Cullen — married!

We had a dinner in the church basement and then held a reception in the village hall which we had decorated ourselves on Christmas Day. It was a big wedding but it wasn't expensive. The wedding cost me about $180. Most people brought food and the hall cost only five bucks. One of the beautiful things about northern Wisconsin people is that so many of them are very handy with their hands. This is especially true of Netty's family. Netty and Catherine and all the girls in the wedding party sewed their own dresses. Even the wedding-cake was home-made, so there were no major expenses.

Netty had dozens of relatives living up there and with all the relatives of her sister Catherine's husband, there were some three hundred people around. That's including the many friends of the four of us who were married. None of my relatives made it.

Netty Rhody is the second of five children of Mr. and Mrs. Carl H. Rhody. Mr. Rhody owns some six hundred acres, much of which is wooded. The Rhody family was not poor, but the stones in the soil and the bad weather do not make for easy living. But the Rhody's are wonderful people. Even though I was a "foreigner" they accepted me completely — and I know they liked me. Even when my radicalism became evident, they stuck with me, basically, even though they could not completely understand. This is not true of all of Netty's relatives — especially some of those who have never forgiven her father for becoming a Catholic.

Our honeymoon wasn't much. We went to Milwaukee! We first lived in a small apartment in Cedarburg, Wisconsin, and I worked in a paint factory there. But I soon got tired of that. I saw I wasn't going anywhere, and I felt that somehow I had to get back into some aspect of nursing. So I started working in the Glendale Nursing Home just north of Milwaukee.

(There I took care of a lot of men and women who were in their late years in life, and couldn't take care of themselves. It was always a tough job, a job which demands people who are sensitive to work with old people. When you see men not able to do the basic things that all of us do, whether it's going to the toilet or eating food, just having to be cared for as if they were children, sensitive people bleed. I remember reading Cicero's *De Senectute* in my Latin class. He talks about old age, and how to deal with it, and his writing left a deep impression on me.)

But even though I enjoyed the work very much and thought it was important, Netty and I felt I had more talent and ability than I was called upon to use. Netty, as good wives do, gave me confidence. She made me believe in myself.

Within a few months after our marriage I made my move to the business world. I entered the race to keep up with the Joneses and only by the grace of God and Father James Groppi did I drop out of the race.

CHAPTER FOUR

As I looked at the business world, I figured that sales would be an interesting field to get into. My best qualification was that I liked people — a qualification every salesman must have to make it.

So, I applied to become a salesman — an insurance salesman. I applied to the Mutual of Omaha Company and within a few weeks I was on my way to Omaha, Nebraska, to study in their sales school.

I had no problem learning the product and I was introduced to the whole American business bit. We had to learn scripts, as if we were going to be in a drama or a play. We were taught to sell — not out of conviction or sincerity, but because of a script we had learned.

They say you will come to believe in the product. Well, I was never short on enthusiasm and I always considered myself a good actor (all the way back to my days in Ireland). Besides, I guess I did believe in what I was doing to a certain extent. I felt at that time insurance was necessary — hospital insurance, life insurance, etc. I reasoned that families could not get along without insurance and therefore, it had to be good and an insurance salesman had to be performing a service.

Besides, I enjoyed selling and I sold a helluva lot of insurance. I was really a worker. Like everything else I had ever done, whether it was preaching Catholicism in Hyde Park in London or running a race at Roscrea, I gave myself completely to the task at hand.

I'd stay out and I'd stay out and I wouldn't come home — until on some days I had made two or three sales. I was doing what the business calls "cold turkey work," and I did my best selling to young nurses and teachers.

65

Sometimes I would just pick a block and knock on each door. I'd figure if I sold to one out of ten I was doing all right. And believe it or not I usually did that well. In a little over a year and a half I sold nearly a million dollars worth of insurance. One night I sold over $500,000 worth.

My love for people and my love for selling sometimes did not help my relationship with my wife. Netty was still working, of course, and everyone knows what a tiring and demanding job nursing is. Well, I remember one time when I promised to be home for her especially prepared six o'clock dinner. I got talking to people and didn't make it home until 2:00 a.m. I soon discovered that Netty was anything but a weak, quiet person. Women's Liberation was a cause of hers long before it became a real movement.

But we made it through those crises and after a year and a half, Tom Collins, a man who was running his own agency, asked me to head up his health and life department. He offered me a fine base pay plus commissions. I took the job and was really beginning to roll. Netty worked until her first pregnancy, so until that time her income helped, too.

But my mind was still alive and active and inquisitive. The broad education I had received would not and could not let me get into too much of a rut. I had collected a good little library, and when I had the chance I had my head into a book.

Then, too, I was doing a lot of selling in the city and Milwaukee was becoming close to me. Then I heard about this guy named Father Groppi.

I remember one black lady to whom I was selling insurance. She told me about this Father Groppi and she said, "I think he's too radical." I asked her what Father Groppi was doing and she told me he had locked himself to a barbwire fence down at the construction site of a new McDowell school — a school which he said was being constructed to perpetuate segregation in the city's public schools.

The whole thing puzzled me and it wouldn't leave me. I kept churning the thing around and around in my mind. One reason it interested me so much is that I used to hear the other salesmen at work speak about staying "out of the jungle." They meant the black community. I didn't know what it was all about, but I recognized the racist statements for what they were and I would be furious and outraged.

At that time, too, I became more aware of Dorothy Day's Catholic Worker Movement. My closest friend, Bob Gilliam, whom I got to know so well in the seminary, was working with Dorothy in New York. I saw clearly that here was a group of people who were really trying to understand and live the Gospel. I read "The Catholic Worker" and I knew how right these people were.

(The Catholic Worker is a *movement* of Christians. It is not like a corporation and you don't have name tags and you don't have a special certificate to show you are a member of the Catholic Worker. In fact, the Catholic Worker is a movement of *radical* Christians. The word "radical" means, "from the roots." It comes from the Latin word, "radix," meaning "root."

Catholic, in my mind, means universal, and I find the early Christians Catholic because they believed in the one-ness and in the uniqueness of mankind. I find the early Christians living what Carl Sandburg meant when he said, there is only one man in the world and he's known as all men, and there's only one woman in the world and her name is all women, and there is only one child and that child's name is all children. And if I find the early Christians living that in a very real sense, standing up for life when it's being destroyed and being maimed and confronted and so forth, then if Catholics are going to be really Catholics, they have to be real Christians, and if Christians are going to be real Christians, in the understanding of Sandburg, they must begin to believe and live that way. For example, no longer can war have any place in our lives, and no longer can violence to human beings have any place in our lives.

Often we fall short of Christianity in many, many ways. For example, no longer do we have an excuse for poverty. No longer do we have an excuse for malnutrition in our world. No longer may we allow our brothers to die of hunger. If we have bread, we must share the same loaf with the poor man. It's better to have both of us die than have one of us die, the other living on the whole loaf. Better to share the loaf and die in the end. That to me is Catholic.

The Catholic Worker was exemplifying, was doing exactly what I am saying. It was started by a man by the name of Peter Maurin, a peasant from France who came to this country. He worked in the lumber yards, in the skid rows of our country, in the odd jobs, a man of the people. Herman who was here in the trial, and Bud and people like them — these are the real people, the people who are considered often by our society to be at the bottom of the ladder, but people we must stand by — because if we don't stand by them, whom do we stand by? If we do not stand with these men, we divide the family of man.

For example, we must see to it that the law provides that the poor will always have legal counsel. The poor make up most of the people who walk our jails. That's a sad mark against this society — and it has to change. The poor need the same counsel I am getting in this trial and the same kind of law, the same quality of fairness that Judge Gordon is giving me. And I say that not just out of deference, but I say it out of respect.

I do not question the legitimacy of a government. I do not question its right to exist. However, I think that legitimacy can often be corrupted. Government can make too many claims. Caesar can have too much. Caesar is not always right. Render to Caesar what is Caesar's, but when Caesar decides to take things that are God's, things which are only God's right and authority, the Christian must say no to those claims. One of these claims is the claim on life. The claim on life is made by Caesar in the form of the draft, mustering men for murder.

Anyway, Peter Maurin was a man of the streets, a great historian, a gentleman, a Christian Brother in France, and when he entered the U.S., he took the lowest place, the lowest paying job in society and walked the roads, and later wrote a book called *Easy Essays*. Then he met a woman by the name of Dorothy Day. Dorothy was going to be here at the trial today, but she is not well at this time. She is seventy-two years of age and not well, although she still does a lot of traveling.

Dorothy Day and Peter Maurin began the Catholic Worker. Dorothy Day was a convert to the Church. She was a Communist, a socialist in the beginning of her life, and later became a Catholic after the birth of her first child. She had just one child, a girl who was born out of wedlock. But the birth of that child made such an important impact upon her life that she said she just naturally became a Christian. It's very hard for us to think that because I am sure she had other influences, but the very gift of giving life, which a woman can give, which nobody else on the planet can give, the gift of another man, another woman for life, was an extraordinary happening in her life, and so she became a Christian, a Catholic.

She started writing books and for magazines like "Commonweal," which is a magazine about Catholic social thought. For example, she covered the Hunger March on Washington of the 1930's. After Dorothy covered this Hunger March, Peter Maurin met her. Peter was one of those people who would talk your ear off, but he always talked about the right things. He had no time for flippant talk. When he spoke, people listened, and he spoke about the things that affected all of us, his life and everybody else's. So he spoke to Dorothy and she got so tired she was hoping he would go away, but he came back the next day and this went on for three months like this. He taught her what being a radical Catholic meant — getting back to the roots, the Gospels, the foundations of our faith — not the heritage of blood-letting, not the heritage of becoming soldiers and taking on the side of the wealthy and never being on the side of the poor, but being on the side of all men. Peter taught Dorothy radical Catholic history, the history of the Church, what the Gospels were about.

So Dorothy found herself compelled. She understood what it was to be a Christian, to go among the poorest of people. First she started publishing the paper called "The Catholic Worker," which was to bring the community of faith, the Catholic Church, into living the Gospels in a real way — feeding the hungry, clothing the naked, sheltering the homeless, visiting the prisoner, being peace-makers and loving your enemy.

These are the tough demands of the Gospels. Simple demands to understand, but tough ones to live. Feed the hungry, share your food. When you have two coats in your closet and the poor man has none, he has a right to the coat because it's really his. Christ Himself says this. All the goods of the earth belong to all the people of the earth.

Then we see Dorothy going into the skid rows, particularly into the Bowery of New York City and opening up a breadline, not just to give food to men out of responsibility, but out of love, out of deep love. And that's the message, you see.

As St. Vincent de Paul said, it's only in the way we give bread to the poor that they forgive us for giving them bread. It's in the way we give it, that we keep dignity alive, that we do it out of love, with the realization that some day we might be like that poor man, the man without a job; that we might be that way now were it not for some great blessing that came our way that we had no control over.

And so, Dorothy Day opened a hospitality house, St. Joseph's Hospitality House, in the Bowery of New York City. She kept publishing her paper which took strong stands on radical pacifism — that Christians in essence were obliged to be pacifists and to be non-violent, not just because we had reached the stage in history where mankind and womenkind could annihilate themselves, as we very definitely can at this time. The Catholic Worker people were saying in 1930 that Christians were obliged to be pacifists by virtue of their being Christians, by their very Baptism. The Baptism of Jesus required us to be non-violent and to be pacifists and to render life, to welcome the enemy — what an insane thing! — and to feed them rather than to kill them. It's an awful demand — to have one's own blood spilled rather than to have someone else's blood spilled. It's better to go to prison, not out of anger for your brother who sent you there, but in the hope that others will see this is where we have to move if we are going to have a history and a future.

This was the heart of the Catholic Worker movement: the clothing and feeding of the poor, the visiting of our brother in prison, seeing him as our brother and sister, as standing for life at all times, wherever and however degraded, to stand on the side of the most depressed and dehumanized, to stand on the side of people victimized on the basis of skin-color and what have you.

Already in the '30's, the Catholic Worker looked at a man as appearing in many colors, like the trees of the autumn here in the state of Wisconsin, a variety of life, a gift. We have gotten away from what we are about, away from America's dream, built upon an ideal. Maybe a few understood — maybe Jefferson understood. Maybe one or two. Maybe Lincoln understood, maybe. . .

How important it is, our rendering of life, seeing life, seeing that all men are created equal. I didn't have to learn that from the American Constitution. I learned that from the Gospels — that we are brothers and sisters of one family. In essence, the early Americans built a nation upon that idea. But that nation has been betrayed! And I'm not here to condemn any person, but I'm here to say the signs are all too visible of the betrayal of that dream that all men are equal, that all men have certain rights. I am sure that the judge and the jury and the defense and the prosecution and everyone here wants this. We must make it possible because that's America's dream, that's the heart of this land. Any one can cross this soil and see that we are a rich land and a rare land, a fresh land and a fair land, this young land of America. But most of the people in this young land in its two and a half centuries of history have been concerned with the making of money and profit rather than living out the dream and rendering to our brothers what they have a right to, be they black brothers, be they Indians whom we found here.

We must acknowledge our own sins, as we say in the language of the Christian, and acknowledge our own faults. We can never move into the history of the future of mankind unless we acknowledge where we have gone wrong. It is important, it is necessary that we can acknowledge it. The Germans went wrong. Hopefully, never will a Dachau be heard of again. Hopefully, we'll never see a slave chain on black men again. We still have the mark of that slavery in this country; the blacks in our central cities, the Indians on our reservations, and poor whites of the mountain regions of Kentucky and the southern states, and the Mexican-Americans, the Puerto Rican Americans who now occupy the poorest parts of our cities, the central parts, the Chicanos, people like Chavez, the migrant workers of the fields, still picking crops for pitiful wages in subhuman conditions to feed the wealthy. That's what we have to acknowledge, and we have to get to the tough task of rebuilding that society.

So, I found this all a part of where I have been coming from and going, you see. I found myself looking at the Catholic Worker and seeing there an articulation of and most of all, a living out, a carrying out of these ideals. As the saying goes, let me see how you live, and I'll tell you who you are.

And so I found myself deeply influenced by Dorothy Day and the Catholic Worker movement. What we call "Catholic Worker Houses" had emerged all over the United States in many cities. There was one here in Milwaukee back in 1942. But 1942 was a tough year. It was the year of the Second World War, and it confronted Americans like they were never confronted before. They began to see a threat to their dream. They began to see a threat to their freedom. That was our mistake. Freedom can never be protected by the barrel of a gun. The centuries of mankind and his history have told man he could not protect freedom by the sword, by napalm or by the greatest hydrogen power we can develop today. We have found that killing brought its own death to all of us in this society. Right now it's tearing our soul. Vietnam has torn the very spirit of us as a young people. We no longer can watch, some of us, the madness of Vietnam and its blood in colored T.V. because we know it's not a movie. We know it's not a movie! It's not a John Wayne western. It's reality. It's 1970. We can no longer watch it or we might go mad.

So, we found ourselves developing a sense of conscience. And I could never have developed this conscience if I had never arrived here. I might still be making hay in Ireland. I might still be living on my father's farm.

But who knows? Judges and juries are not important. Most important is that we are and we be the best kind of men and women we can possibly be. That's the most important thing. Justice has always been our pride. We must do what we know is the right thing for us. That's the most important thing. That's how history is made and changed for the betterment of man.)

So my head began radically changing. Just when I became a manager and had my greatest chance of being "successful" and of building a real future! I knew I could do it — if I just would not become socially involved.

I was getting tired of our parish. I offered my services many times, but the pastor kept putting me off. Finally, I decided to go to Milwaukee for Mass on Sunday. First we went to St. Nicholas on the north side and I even began teaching freshmen C.C.D.; that is, giving religious instruction. I even gave a couple of retreats. A retreat is a time spent by a group of people who wish to be renewed spiritually by listening to a preacher and by praying. It is extraordinary then that I as a layman was called upon to do this.

Then my son, Willie, was born. It was February 16, 1966, and I remember looking out at the fresh snow falling and trying to grasp the full implication of being a father. Willie began to press hard on me. Now I had to choose between building a future for him and that toward which my head was beginning to turn. Now I had to think of providing a future, not just for Netty and myself, but for Willie. I had to think of a safe home in a good community and of Willie's education.

But the problems I saw in the city were always confronting me. I was gradually becoming convinced that we had to build a future not by making money but by developing our lives in terms of social concerns.

71

As I continued reading "The Catholic Worker," I began wondering if I could begin a Catholic Worker community. So I started having meetings at our house to discuss the Catholic Worker philosophy. That's how I met John Rowan who later became a director of a poverty program on the south side of Milwaukee.

Also, Pat Hagarty and Bob Phelps became close friends. They had a small apartment down near Father Groppi's base at St. Boniface in Milwaukee.

So, I began coming down to St. Boniface and hearing Father Groppi rap about injustice. I would be out selling insurance every day but at 7:00 p.m. I was down at St. Boniface for Mass. I never missed a day. That was the real beginning of indoctrination and radicalization.

Father Groppi would talk about the injustice, the poverty of the city and the racism in the schools. He read things from Dr. Martin Luther King, Jr.

(But it was during this time that when I left for work in the morning I had to admit my thoughts were not on my work as much as on what I'd be doing that night — catching Father Groppi's Mass at St. Boniface Church. Father Groppi was doing things to my head that people I had met in the past had done, people like the saints, people like Jefferson, people like Thomas Aquinas and Thomas More, people like Martin King. Jim Groppi was doing the same thing to me. He was challenging my faith. Was I living it or was I not? Was it all a kind of nice romantic talk or was it real? Was I willing to put myself out on behalf of others? I found him challenging me on the problem of racism, the things that began to bother me the first three years in the seminary. Martin King was not going to eliminate racism alone. He needed everybody and we needed to get to the task. It's like Gandhi. Everyone says Gandhi was a failure because he didn't wipe out the poverty of India, the most impoverished country today. But that's our problem. We must see these men only as a beginning. We must see Christ as a beginning. We must see Gandhi as a beginning. They are inviting you and me, all of us, to do in a like manner.

Father Groppi was inviting me, and I found myself looking more deeply at poverty within the city.)

Jim Groppi and I liked each other from the beginning. I don't know what his early recollections of me are, but we seemed to strike up a very real personal relationship.

We started having the Catholic Worker meetings in an old apartment building near St. Boniface on 10th Street. I told Jim Groppi one day that we were looking for a house so that we could move into the city. At that same time Jim was looking for a Freedom House, so we looked together.

We brought Willie to St. Boniface to be baptized. Father Groppi offered the Mass and Father Mike Neuberger did the baptizing. It was a great baptism. We did it before the noon Mass and destroyed the whole Mass schedule. But we knew we could baptize Willie only if the community was there — so that the people would know that Willie was entering the community and that he was their responsibility.

The baptism started outside on the streets, with the people on the streets, and we sang and we read from the Old and New Testament. A couple of friends and I composed the liturgy. We had some real love songs. Sister Germaine Habjen, who at that time was a Glenmary nun and locally famous as a composer and guitarist-singer, helped brighten the occasion. The whole thing was that Willie was being born into a new life.

And all of us were being born into new life — Netty and I and that whole group who were focusing around Catholic Worker philosophy. We had talked enough. We knew we needed to move. We had to do something — soon.

We discovered that an obvious, real and immediate need in the city of Milwaukee was a shelter for homeless families. Father John Maurice, the founder and long-time director of the Spanish Center on the south side of Milwaukee, was anxious to have us do something to fill that need.

We discovered that the old Guadalupe church was going to be vacated because the parish was going to merge with Holy Trinity parish. We decided to rent the Guadalupe rectory from the diocese. We didn't know how we were going to run the center but we formed a Board of Directors.

We needed someone who knew his way around the legal matters. Luckily, we had E. Michael McCann, a man I had met and became a close friend of when both of us were attending pre-cana conferences as we prepared for marriage.

Mike was a very religious guy. He had been a seminarian for a couple of years and developed a deep love for the Church. He had also visited Ireland and loved it.

We had a close relationship. Mike was always available. Anytime I wanted to do something, he was always there. He was very happy to handle the legal matters involved in incorporating our Catholic Worker House. He was also one of the first members of our Board of Directors.

But then the project got more and more political and Mike McCann began to retreat — because he was beginning his own political career. He had his sights on becoming the District Attorney of Milwaukee County, and, of course, he made it. As things began to happen in my life, it got so that Mike could not or would not even talk with me. What a tragedy.

But I love Mike McCann and I still think he's a good guy. I can't be judgmental. A very human guy. Mike always had a great love for

Thomas More and in every situation he would ask himself what Thomas More would do. Well. . .

Meanwhile, Father Jim Groppi kept getting deeper and deeper inside of me. It wasn't just what Jim was talking about. It suddenly became obvious that his work was exactly what the Church is all about. Very obvious! Suddenly I saw that the Gospel is very simple. No genius is necessary to see that the Gospel condemns racism. The Gospel tells us our obligation to the poor.

And the liturgies, the Masses we celebrated at St. Boniface became more and more meaningful. Mass was celebrated there in an informal setting and it was more real, more human, and people were acting more humanly. Usually, not too many people were there, and we all came up around the altar and we could all say what we felt. The Spirit was truly alive with us and we celebrated Mass with great joy and much growth. We all felt a real kinship, a tremendous fellowship — and I guess we sort of inspired each other.

As my friendship with Jim Groppi grew, I found him a hard-headed individual. He's very stubborn — always very stubborn. He is a leader, he can dominate, and that's what makes him what he is.

But what most people don't know is that Jim Groppi is a very gentle man. He is also a man of tremendous faith. His belief in the Gospels is very, very real — even more real now after what he's been through.

But he never wore his faith on his sleeve, especially in the beginning. He never talked about Jesus in rallies and rarely explicitly related the civil rights cause to religion or to a religious issue.

I was still an insurance man, but I must have walked in every one of Father Groppi's marches. And oh, God, when I look back on those days — wow! The bottles and the Molotov cocktails! I mean we really went into the heart of the revolution.

It was not easy relating to black people because I felt what black people felt for white people — that all white people — liberals — intrude. And I was outraged inside when I was looked at in this way because I was not an American. At least I did not consider myself an American racist. I was an immigrant and I knew what poverty was and I knew what exploitation was, and it was not in keeping with my tradition to choose between men on the basis of race.

The blacks were my brothers and sisters and I wanted to be there as much as anybody. And so, I threw myself into the whole question. It was the right thing to do. It was not the coerced thing to do out of fear. It was the right thing to do and I had to do it.

I remember the night we were to march to the south side of Milwaukee for the first time. I arrived there with this big crucifix and said, "Jim, we're going to use this tonight." And he said, "Oh, no!" He sort of embarrassed me because I wasn't one of those Jesus-stricken people, and I didn't want to be either.

But I wanted to say that we had the sign of crucifixion and I thought we should use it. But then we had some reservations. Perhaps someone might grab it and use it for a weapon. Maybe Jim was afraid of that, too.

Anyway, I went into the Freedom House with the crucifix and I put it behind the door. It was a terrible, terrible night. We really did not think we were going to come out of it alive. When we got to Lincoln Avenue we were sure we were going to be killed.

The violence was so incredible! The streets were filled with so much hate. The bottles that were thrown, the fear, the hate, the spitting. It was a disease! It was as if the whole city had just vomitted, as if everything that was sick in us was being vomitted on the street as we walked.

The people spit on us, they threw rocks and bottles. We used our coats to cover our heads, but one girl was hurt by a molotov cocktail.

I was praying my rosary all the time. I always took my rosary along on those marches because that's the only thing I'm going to die with.

It was a diseased night — but a great night. It was the real beginning of the liberating of our heads and our spirits. We began to see what we had to do, what lay ahead for us, what the future held in store.

Anyhow, by some miracle, we got back to the Freedom House. We thought nothing more was going to happen and so we went home.

When I arrived back home, I hadn't even gotten into the house when a call came saying the Freedom House was on fire. We went back immediately, and was the place blazing! The streets were all lined off. There must have been some two hundred and fifty police all over the place. Incredible times!

The next day someone took the burnt crucifix — my crucifix — and hung it on the outside of the Freedom House. I thought I would let it there for a few days and then I'd pick it up and bring it home. But I never got it. Someone must have it as a relic.

But the charred crucifix, the charred Christ, the charred cross — what a symbol for those times — for our times!

Of course, the next night we went again to the south side, and the same madness went on, the same insanity. When we got back to the Freedom House, again the police were swarming the place. That was the first night I witnessed real police violence. I'll never forget some two hundred policemen coming up the street with their bayonets and their guns and their sticks and their blue helmets — they looked like blue devils out of hell. The people were aghast. The police started swinging at our feet, telling us to get on the sidewalk.

75

Then a policeman read some kind of declaration, telling us that we all had to go home, that we had to get off the streets. Then, all of a sudden, without warning, they charged the Freedom House. The fear, the screaming, the insanity! That night, hell was a place called Milwaukee.

These were my first experiences with a society deeply ill and disturbed. And it was Jim Groppi who opened my eyes. Already in those days our lives were tied. The funny thing is I never got arrested with Jim. I never got arrested in those demonstrations. Many times the opportunity was there, but I never got picked up.

One night we were forbidden to march but we did anyway. Almost everyone in the group got picked up. I just stood there and started writing down badge numbers. The paddy-wagon took off and there I was, standing out on the sidewalk.

But Jim is a real friend, a guy I have a tremendous amount of respect for, a gentle friend, a truly human person, a guy deeply disturbed by the Gospels. I think Jim's deepest motivation is the Gospel — more than anything else, more than any political philosophy.

It's certainly true that Jim has gotten angry. Often this anger comes across as if it's violent and sometimes he's not careful with his words. But Jim's been through some real struggles — the whole thing about letting blacks do it for themselves. His experiences in jail really shook him up. I believe non-violence is becoming something positive for him.

Not that Jim Groppi would have ever taken up a gun. I'm positive of that. But now he, like the rest of us, is beginning to see the need to develop the possibilities of non-violence. How do we bring new imagination to non-violence? To be non-violent, one has to be creative. Violence does not demand creativity.

In the United States the non-violent person will have to be especially creative. Given the fact of who our enemy is and the equipment and ammunition the enemy has — wow! How do we conduct guerilla warfare in a non-violent way?

There's a spiritual poverty in this society. Non-violence is a spiritual weapon. Martin King was beginning to understand this. I think Chavez is a great help. Resistance, yes, and boycotts, but more than this.

Real change is needed. We can't just become a part of society, making it, so that we do the same kind of exploiting and become part of the same corruption. We dare not just move into society as many labor unions have done. We dare not think of high salaries and fringe benefits if they are at the expense of others — and they usually are.

We must speak more about co-ops, as Chavez has done. We must give the land back to the people. We must speak of medical clinics. We must talk about a whole new style of society.

76

So I'm saying Jim Groppi and others like him had to begin to do these things. Perhaps only men with faith will be able to accomplish these things. Jim Groppi has faith. He keeps reading the Scriptures. He carried the Scriptures to Madison with the welfare mothers — the time he "took over" the capitol. When he was in jail he admitted that the only way he survived was by praying his breviary, his rosary, and by reading the Bible. These were his means of keeping sane, of staying alive, of maintaining hope.

I can say the same thing about my first jail experience. If a person interrupts the status quo, if a person causes trouble which is socially unacceptable, he needs an added strength. The true Christian has this — and this is why he has an added task, a bigger responsibility — to work for the poor, the outcast, or to be a peacemaker.

Jim Groppi has been a guy who never caused trouble that was socially acceptable. He caused the right kind of trouble. He rattled people's consciences. He was swimming upstream when everyone else was coming down. And that's the only thing we as Christians can do. That's what the times demand. As Christians we have to become men and women who stand apart from the system. We are very critical of our culture, of religion, of politics. For this we are ostracized. For this we are not understood. We may not act in the most diplomatic way, but we're not interested in diplomacy. We are interested in truth. We're interested in justice. We're interested in the right thing to be done.

And we dare not sit around waiting. We cannot wait until all the analysis is done, though analysis there must be. In the face of obvious injustice, the Christian must act — even though he is not altogether sure of the consequences of his actions.

Jim Groppi acted — although he had no idea that jail would be as hard for him as it was. The guy was really breaking up inside, really having a hard time dealing with it. And yet, right after he got out of jail, he couldn't remain silent. He had to talk about the injustice there. He described jail as "a sadistic act of vengeance of a morally sick society."

He called me the day he got out of jail and asked me to come over. After he read his own archbishop's condemnation of his actions, he said he felt like taking off his collar and taking his Bible and going to see the Archbishop. He said he wanted to knock on his door and say, "Archbishop, here's my Jesus collar and my Jesus book. It's been too much for me. You try it. I'm going to get a job."

Really, this is tough stuff — living the Jesus life, trying to understand who he is, as a man and as God, and to talk about justice and to do things you really don't understand yourself. You wonder just why in hell you're in jail, why in hell you're doing what you're doing. You know

77

very well you could be living a half-way decent life somewhere in the world.

And all the time the same answer comes back. We are Christians and what we are doing is the right thing to do. We don't need any other excuse. But in my own life, and in the lives of guys like Groppi, King, Chavez, etc., the deepest motivation is faith.

The man of faith really has to do what he sees must be done or his faith is empty and meaningless. The man of faith has vision. He is able to cut through the rhetoric and the fear and say yes. He's able to say, "I'm afraid, scared as hell, but it must be done."

And so, you look at the words of Jesus and he says feed the hungry. And you know that is what you must do. People tell you, well it's nice to feed the hungry but you shouldn't be feeding them in this neighborhood. We don't want the bum and the panhandler in this neighborhood.

And you become outraged and angry, but you go on feeding the hungry because it's God's law and to stop feeding the hungry is to break God's law. If a man is hungry, you don't turn him away. You don't sit around to talk about it. You feed the man. The people in the neighborhood may try to run you out, burn you out, or even try to kill you. But you go on doing God's law.

That's what my faith is all about. That's what Jesus exemplifies. There's no more Greek or Roman or Jew or Gentile. We are all brothers and there is only one man and one woman and one child as Sandburg says.

My dear mother in Ireland had taught me all of this and I saw it lived in her. My training in the faith, my reading of the Scriptures, the lives of the Saints, my study of theology — all of this prepared me.

But it was Father Jim Groppi who provided the spark that lit the flame.

CHAPTER FIVE

The philosophy of the Catholic Worker movement was already operating in our lives, long before the group of us got serious about a shelter for homeless families.

But now it was time to do something. Mike McCann, a member of the group, began proceedings to incorporate the Catholic Worker House as a legitimate organization of the state of Wisconsin. We weren't at all sure just what we were incorporating, but we felt it was the right thing to do. I believe we felt that if a hospitality house evolved, it would be just one part of a larger movement.

Father Maurice had told us of the need for a shelter for migrant families. Another man, Jesus Pagan (in Spanish that name comes off all right, but in English!) kept telling us of this tremendous need.

There was a house next to an old church which once was a post office. The church used to be Our Lady of Guadalupe and it served the Spanish-Americans who had moved into the area. Another church, also an ethnic parish called Holy Trinity, was close by. Since the Holy Trinity church had very few parishioners left, the diocese closed down Our Lady of Guadalupe and combined it with Holy Trinity.

Anyway, the rectory of Our Lady of Guadalupe was empty and the diocese had no plans for it. We found we could rent it for $100.00 a month. The diocese paid for the electricity and the gas.

Now all we needed was for someone to move in and take charge. Netty and I felt we were still free enough in our lives to do this. We were not bound to the economic slavery of this society. Besides, we felt it was the right thing to do.

But we had no blueprint to say how to set up the house. The Catholic Worker movement in New York City was basically serving Bowery men and Skid Row men. They were not dealing with families and this was all very new for us. This would have to be a very new kind of community, a different kind of house. The only thing we knew is that we would move in and live there.

We moved in in late August, 1966. It was here that my real Baptism took place. The abstract now became concrete.

I continued on as insurance salesman because I didn't know how I was going to get income. There was no money given to us as a salary — from anybody, and that includes the diocese. Basically, Netty and I felt that we were called to serve.

That serving would be mainly to migrant workers. Migrant workers, usually Mexican-American from the deep South, are very visible in northern Wisconsin in the fall as they are in many states. The salaries of these seasonal workers are absurdly low in terms of the travel and time spent not working. Often the families have not earned enough money to travel back to their homes in southern Texas.

The poverty of the migrant camps has been exposed time and time again but little or nothing is done about it. Some of the migrants come into the city to escape that poverty but often end up even further disillusioned. They are often not at all equipped to live in the city, let alone possess the skills necessary to earn a decent living.

And so we found these migrant families sleeping in cars along the lake front or in abandoned cars. Or we found them in abandoned and condemned houses. Often they didn't have a chance to make a beginning, sometimes merely because they didn't have the money to pay the first month's rent. How does a man get a job when he is looking for a place to live? And how does one pay rent until the first pay check comes?

All of this would be difficult enough but there was or is the added problem of the language barrier. It is difficult to deal with the enormity of this problem since it lies outside of the experience of most of us.

Moving day finally came for Netty and me and Willie. A friend let us use his truck to haul the furniture we had in Cedarburg. The stuff was scattered all over our "new" home, but we were so tired we went to bed at 11:00.

About 1:00 a.m. there was a knock at the door. A woman who could speak no English made it clear to us that she needed a place to stay. I couldn't believe it! How was it possible? Who told her about us?

The house, a former rectory for some four or five priests, had four major bedrooms and another large room we made into a bedroom. My wife and the baby and I occupied only one room.

There was no furniture in the place. The priests took it all with them. But we began collecting things, especially mattresses and beds.

Because one thing's for sure, the Spanish-Americans came, just as we had been told they would. From that first night on they came and they kept right on coming.

Neither Netty nor I could speak Spanish but what came across was that we are all human beings, brothers and sisters. We didn't have to speak words to let people know that we really cared, that we were deeply concerned, that we were very happy to give them shelter, that our house was truly an open house, open to anyone and everyone at all times.

I'm not sure when we got down to the business of finding a name for our house. The group of us had a meeting and agreed that the name should have something to do with the Mexican-American, Spanish-American culture. For centuries now, Mary, the Mother of Christ, has been such a part of that culture. We decided that we'd call the house the house of Mary — Casa Maria.

We kept that name, even when we moved to another house and even though we served people of all nationalities and religions. The name gave us an identity and before long, reporters were coming around and Casa Maria became known to the city of Milwaukee. One story by Ethel Gintoft, which appeared in the Milwaukee archdiocesan newspaper, "The Catholic Herald Citizen," was reprinted in a small Catholic magazine, "The Precious Blood Messenger," and also in "The Catholic Digest."

And so, in a few short months, we were known to the nation, and though we could hardly believe that such a small effort, such a small Christian venture should get such publicity, we were deeply grateful. We needed all the support we could get.

The publicity also showed us that people are attracted by the Gospels, that living the Gospels was not a complicated, theological matter, that it took no great mind to see the rightness of sheltering the homeless and feeding the hungry.

But, as had to be expected, different people had different ideas as to how Casa Maria was to be run. Some thought the house should become a center for mobilizing the Mexican-Americans. Some thought the house should be a very traditionally governed house, serving a specific function — much like an agency of some kind.

But Netty and I had our own ideas about Casa Maria. I was just beginning to really move with the Gospel. The Gospel was very much permeating my reason for living in Casa Maria. For example, I wanted no part of a salary for working at Casa Maria, for serving the poor. It didn't make any sense to me. I began to feel a real call to voluntary poverty.

Hence, I felt it very necessary to beg for our food. I felt it was necessary to involve the community, the Christian community, the whole community. The community had to have a part in our work, a real part, a real personal involvement — not just by way of giving money to some special fund. The Gospels demand, the Gospels DEMAND that the Christian serve the poor by feeding him and clothing him and right from the beginning that was operating in my head.

Well, the first night this lady arrived (she turned out to be from Colombia, South America) and the next day three Mexican-American migrant workers arrived from Texas. They thought the place was a joke! They couldn't believe it. At first they were afraid and they stayed in their room. I was busy cleaning up the place — it needed so much work — cleaning and painting, etc.

All of a sudden they couldn't stand it any more. The three big guys decided to come down and help. They said they just couldn't believe the place. There had to be a catch. They were sure they were being taken by someone, that they had fallen into another trap.

But the fear and distrust soon disappeared and this became a pattern for Casa Maria. From the beginning we were a house with an open door and we made it clear that we were there only because we wanted to be there. And we were open, not just to those in need of food and shelter, but to the whole community, to all the people in the neighborhood.

People began bringing us food and supplies. We made sure it wasn't just for those at Casa Maria. It was given to anyone who asked for it. So very soon we got to know not only the families who came to us for shelter but many other families in the neighborhood and in the larger community.

And there as we moved into the cold Milwaukee winter, we began to know the men on National Avenue, many of whom were alcoholics, living in empty and meaningless vacuums known as rooming houses. Many of them were veterans living on small pensions like $70.00 a month, not nearly enough to make it. Many of these men were locked out of their rooms because they couldn't meet the rent. They needed a place — it was that simple and the Christian has only one way to respond.

Before long then, the real poor found us, the poorest people in the whole city and this is what radicalized me! I cannot stress that fact enough — I was radicalized finally and irrevocably by the poor, by my daily and living encounter with the dispossessed, the hungry, the homeless, the cold, the lost, the afraid, the lost — the real people of God.

Daily I was overwhelmed by the people desperately in need of help, people with nowhere to go, even though there were dozens of agencies, even though the government was supposedly waging a multi-million dollar war on poverty, even though "the Church" and the churches and synagogues had abundant wealth and thousands of rooms in rectories and convents and parsonages which were empty and unused — and warm.

82

So many people come to mind. I remember the American Indian wife who came with her children. Her husband had been jailed for robbery. We stuck with that woman and her children, and her husband came back out of jail, and we found them a home and they're making it.

(Now, this was a very major transition that took place as a result of my life in the hospitality house, and our lives, my wife and myself, and those who joined us, because of our actual contact with poverty. Though I had come out of a heritage of poverty, it was still abstract because of the privileges I had had in this society, of going to school and living a safe life — safe in the sense that I had sufficient money always to provide for my family. But now we became quite vulnerable to all that the poor meet on a daily basis, the uncertainty, the having to beg and share our bread. We felt as Catholic Worker people have always felt, people who worked in the Catholic Worker movement, people like Dorothy Day and Peter Maurin, people who have marked the Catholic Worker over the last thirty-five years, that the job of the Christian is to take his place at the side of the poorest people to begin not just to defend the poor but to begin to become like them, realizing one may never really be like them because he has had many privileges and he has chosen to be poor while the real poor are there by accident or by circumstance. The choice, of course, is the big difference.

It wasn't long before I was asking serious questions. Why did this kind of poverty exist? It was really incredible, the kind of experiences that took place in our lives in a very, very short span of time. For about the first nine months, we saw as many as thirty-five people right here in Milwaukee come to our door on a daily basis who needed shelter, who needed clothing, who needed food — the things that we would just absolutely take for granted as a people in this society. To my amazement, there were needy people in this rich land. I remember in the beginning I used to wonder if people were kidding us, if the poor themselves were kidding us. This couldn't be real.

I began to see the inadequacies of the welfare system at that time. In 1966, the welfare law stated that a person had to be in the state of Wisconsin at least one year before he could get welfare benefits. Now that excluded many of the poor, of course, and particularly, the migrant worker who was here maybe just for a season. And if jobs are bad, if the harvest fails, he can't make any money, he is really stuck. The family is stuck. And so he either has to beg or make his way back to his native state.

We came across one family with twelve children in a south side apartment in the winter of 1966-67. The youngest child was about six weeks old and had recently caught pneumonia. This family was in the state of Wisconsin only about eight months and hence could get no welfare help. The father of the family had apparently abandoned them by

83

joining the army or something. The mother was stuck with the children. We were able to provide some help, of course, but the enormity of this burden on us in addition to the people who came on a daily basis was just too much. We finally went to the state and here's what the state people did: they gave the mother $50.00 and put the family on a train for their native state of California.

So I began asking questions — not only about the welfare system which since then has changed somewhat, but about the very nature of our country. In regards to welfare laws and many other laws it became apparent that we are not really the "United" States but rather, we are like fifty separate countries.

I began to ask why people, the real poor, had difficulty getting welfare payments when I or any other more fortunate person, who had been employed for a period of time and got laid off could go down to the Unemployment office and get some money. What is this but another kind of welfare? Why is one more shameful than the other? Why do the more fortunate get more help than the poorest of the poor?

It seems to me that if we are going to be a people who really feel for life, then we must revere and respect people at the lowest point in the ladder. They too have rights and we have a duty to share with them the skills and protections that all the people in the Union are able to have, be they rich or poor.

In the winter of 1966 we turned our basement into a sort of flop house. We had about fourteen men at a time, mostly alcoholics, men who couldn't make it on their puny $100.00, poor men who had to buy at the same stores that the rich buy. Under these circumstances it becomes almost impossible to remain human and it's no wonder that you find crime and robbery. It's no wonder that you find a great amount of inhumanity among the poor because the circumstances of their lives lend to this kind of despair. This is what happens when they don't have the human rights that some of us take for granted.

These are some of the clear things that were coming across as I began to see thirty-five people a night looking for shelter and food, men of skid row and all that entangles their lives and makes their lives the way they have turned out to be. There are measures we have never been able to meet, measures that most societies have a hard time with. But we could, it seems to me, if we really tried. If we can go to the moon, certainly we can begin to deal with poverty. I don't say that by way of political speech, I say it because I think we have the capability of doing what I am saying and we must do it if we are going to move into the future.)

Casa Maria's daily contact with the poor radicalized not only me. The same thing was happening to Netty. Her day by day, hour by hour encounter was much harder on her than the whole experience was for me. I was gone a great deal of the time and it was Netty who bore the heaviest burden. She continued her nursing work, sometimes working night hours.

And, of course, she was more concerned with Willie, more worried about his present home and about his future. And then it wasn't long before she was pregnant with Brennan.

Some nights we had over forty people in the house. Sometimes — many times — the house was just wall-to-wall mattresses, with people sleeping anywhere and everywhere.

I took some of the money we had saved up and began putting up some partitions in the basement for the single men. I simply didn't know what else I could do. I couldn't leave anybody out on the streets. I didn't care who they were — we found room for them.

But after about nine months of this, I could feel nerves beginning to crack, mine and Netty's and other people's. The constant drain, the constant strain — we began to feel completely drawn out and suddenly, all that energy that had governed us and prodded us on was slipping away from us. What a frightening thing to know, as a young man or as a young woman, that there is an end to one's energy, that there comes a time when he cannot go on the way he used to be able to do.

After five months I realized I couldn't go on with my job. I was selling very little insurance and we were running out of money. The immediacy of the needs of the people who came to Casa would not permit me to walk around them and go to my job. The work at Casa was much more vital and it had to go on, it had to be done.

So we started begging for money. I started going to churches to beg for money to buy food. One day, a Sunday, Netty went to a church on the north side and I went to the cathedral. I used a basket and I asked the people to feed the hungry, to clothe the naked, to shelter the homeless, to help Casa Maria to do these things. I collected some $40.00.

Netty didn't do so well. She went to St. Robert's and just as Mass was ending she went to the front of the church, even before the priest left the altar and without asking anyone's permission, stood before the 1500 people and said, "I'm Netty Cullen and we need money. We've got seven children at our house and they don't have any milk or food. We need money and want you to give us money. I'll be standing outside in the front of the church with a basket."

The people of St. Robert's were outraged! How dare that woman do that! What gall! How rude and impolite can people be!

But the people of St. Robert's were not nearly so angry as Netty was! She came home furious with $6.00. She just couldn't believe it and she said she would never go back!

85

But we continued on — and wow, the kind of people we attracted. Though Casa Maria was really a home for the homeless, a house for the poorest people of Milwaukee, all kinds of people came to us from all kinds of places. I remember a woman, a divorced or separated woman with eight kids, who was ready for an insane asylum. I don't know what her mind was like before she had the eight children, but at this time the pressures had completely broken her down. She would get up at 5:00 a.m. and start screaming at the top of her voice. Then someone, perhaps a neighbor, would call the police, and it made getting any sleep pretty impossible. But just the thought that this woman and her children were living in our society and no one had come to their help really blows your mind!

One day a man arrived who told us he had just gotten out of jail, a man whom society would label an ex-con. It made no difference to me who he was. Our house was open and no further decisions had to be made as to who was allowed to come in. Anyway, he asked if he could stay around and I said sure, and gave him some work to do. He started working and worked well. Then all of a sudden one day he appeared with a Roman collar on. "Oh, yeah," he said, "I'm a Baptist minister."

Well, I didn't quite know what that meant, but there was no reason to throw him out. Then we discovered that he was wearing his collar and going out into the community getting things in the name of Casa Maria.

At this same time a Milwaukee book publisher brought us this guy who was writing a book on the streets. Well, what could I say, but OK. But this guy was totally disarming. He just fell on top of you with his enthusiasm and embraced you. He was over six feet tall, and, of course, none of us had ever seen him before. We figured this guy had to be out of his mind, but incredibly enough, he really was writing a book and did have two books published. One book was composed of contemporary prayers of the streets.

Well, this Baptist and this author, who was supposedly Catholic, became fast friends and in just a few weeks, the author was ordained a minister by the minister in a back bedroom of our house!

Now the two of them were going out into the community with Roman collars on! They began setting up something for the youth in the neighborhood — something to attract all the kids who had run away from home or were in the process of running away. The author-minister had a fantastic rapport with the kids. He was just an enormously attractive fellow. His enthusiasm and his voice overwhelmed the kids and he really had a poet's heart.

Well, before too long I found out that the first Baptist minister was on drugs and we finally had to commit him to a mental institution. The author-minister finally split for California.

I relate these things to show that there is nothing romantic and pretty about serving the dispossessed, society's castoffs, the people whom society ignores and hopes will go away. I tell these things to show the incredible madness that a place like Casa attracted and will always attract.

We had another young man, also an "ex-con" who was just incredible. He caused tremendous violence in the short time he was with us. One night he raped one of the girls in the neighborhood. The girl's boyfriend came over with a gun and was determined to kill the rapist.

I jumped in between the two and for the first time in my life I faced a loaded revolver. I told the man he would have to shoot me first if he was going to kill anyone. I looked down the barrel of that gun and I knew darn well that it could go off any moment, that this guy was mad enough to pull the trigger. I couldn't believe this was really happening. Why was I being so damn brave? Was this really where my life had taken me?

I started rapping with the guy. I knew I had to talk to him. Finally he handed the gun to me and he started bawling his head off. The whole thing was incredible!

I got out into the night air and walked a couple of blocks with that loaded gun in my pocket. How could it be that my life could be touched in this way in so short a time? It overwhelmed me to realize that the world comes down on top of you in a house like Casa Maria — the whole world!

As time went on, the wealth of inadequacies of the law regarding the poor kept pressing down on me. I was beginning to understand, not theoretically but by my daily contact, why there was so much poverty in the city, why there was so much unemployment, why so many men were unskilled. Society doesn't see the woman or the man or the family who get caught in between the laws and who are unable to get help — immediately — now.

I met a man, for example, who had been in the army for fourteen years and suddenly had to get out and because he had to get out he is unable now to get any decent pension. And so this man has to beg, has to panhandle.

How degrading to see a woman whose husband is in jail out begging for her support, begging to stay alive. She has no skills, no education, and she has to become a street walker. And she's got children. What does she do to feed them?

These are the things society prefers not to see but we were seeing them and experiencing them in every sense of the word. Anyone who came to our house ate at our table, whether individuals or families. That was not always an easy thing. What we were doing was new, new to us and we couldn't look to anyone else to find out what to do and how to do it. We had to follow our own blueprint.

We tried always to make the house a real home. We tried to welcome all as if they were our real brothers and sisters or relatives or friends. The sense of the human family was very real to us.

And we knew at Casa Maria that we were merely dealing with the symptoms or the results of the evils in society. We knew that we were not solving any great problems. We knew we had to deal with the symptoms, that the Christian could not wait until the revolution to promise to feed someone or to give him clothing. The Christian cannot wait for the society to change totally. The Christian responsibility is to feed your brother now, when he is hungry, not after the revolution. You give what you have, you share your bread, you walk a mile — the mandate of the Gospels is either real or it isn't.

Christ told us that the man with two cloaks must give one to the man who had none. The drive toward voluntary poverty was most compelling. Netty and I did possess a few things. And yet we were free, more than most people were. Leaving our own home was the first death, the first stripping, the first step. (I must confess that in my own life my being away from my home in Ireland, from my family and culture, with no idea of what the future held in store was a real baptism toward poverty.)

But Netty and I did have our books, a stereo, a television set, a couple of couches and a bed — and all of a sudden these things came to be used by everyone in the house. And before you can really ask whether these things belong to everybody you have already answered: of course they belong to everybody!

Once a hospitality house was open to everybody, then, of course, everything in that house was open to everybody. Besides, the poor would not permit us to have very much. We ended up with one room because there simply wasn't any more space. Of course, this kind of baptism was the best thing that could have happened to us. We came to realize that we really didn't need much for ourselves.

I remember that I used to keep a lot of books upstairs because I was afraid some of them would be stolen. I was still possessed by those books. That's the problem with possessions — they possess you — you don't possess them! Suddenly it occurred to me — what the hell am I doing with all those books up there? I had read most of them. Why not bring them downstairs so that the community could use them?

And so I was becoming dispossessed by the poor. Our situation was still a raw situation. It was as if the poor had pulled the whole skin off in one day — no, not just the skin, but big hunks of flesh with it.

Many people have tried voluntary poverty, for example religious nuns, brothers and priests in the Roman Catholic tradition. But so often this was a practice, a discipline entirely abstract and unreal.

But there at Casa, my wife and I were thrust right into living poverty. Suddenly all of the things we had belonged to the community. Suddenly all of the things we used to think important in our lives were being used by everybody else and we began to recognize that they were not very important at all. "Losing" the possessions to the community was a great liberating process. We were much freer and more mobile. We were no longer slaves to materialism, to property.

People become slaves to their work, to their cars. Sometimes two people occupy a whole house, a huge house. They don't need all that space, and besides, they waste half of their time cleaning the place when they could be out doing better things.

We so easily become slaves. And what a waste of property, what a waste of material things. We even become slaves to buying — buying things that we don't need and don't even want.

The big question that always bothers people concerns my children. Didn't Netty and I worry about their future, about putting money away for their education?

Well, of course, we did and still do. There was Willie and there was my wife pregnant with Brennan. Were we doing the right thing? It brings up the whole question as to whether any parent has helped his children by handing them things, by showering them with all they need and more. Is this really loving your children?

Aren't there higher values to give your children — the strong and deep example of Christianity — not the Christianity learned from Catechism alone, but rather a Christianity lived and daily present in their lives?

Besides, faith teaches us to trust, that if we do what is right and live Christian lives, we need not fear for the future.

Willie was about nine months, almost ten when we moved to Casa. First of all, a child is better able to adapt to a new environment than any adult. I'm convinced that Willie grew up and matured better in Casa than had he been reared in some suburban home with no one around but a doting mother. He simply was no problem whatsoever.

And he made such a difference in the house. First of all, children are irresistible to everyone — even to the most hardened street man or alcoholic. Willie was always able to make the most depressed and down-and-out man smile again.

Secondly, by being married and having children, we were *real* people to those who came to us. We weren't nuns or priests running the place, good people, but nonetheless difficult if not impossible to identify with. We were a family and people always thought of us as a family. The poor had no trouble relating to us as a family. Most of them had children themselves and the nostalgic memory of the basic needs and the problems of a family was very much a fact of their lives. Often their own families were broken and had very little natural rhythm left in them. But our family was a source of joy and consolation to them. Willie, to put it very briefly, added to our credibility.

So did the fact that we didn't get salaries. Many of the poor were overwhelmed by this and found it difficult to believe. The poor are used to being conned, used to being taken, used to believing there's a gimmick, But there was none and the poor became our real friends.

It was a good thing that the poor befriended us. The people I used to think were such close friends in Cedarburg no longer came to visit us. Neither did the "friends" I made in the insurance business, nor the "friends" Netty had while in nursing school and after. None of them came, and it really blew Netty's mind. She had really believed they were close friends.

And so there was a stripping, a dying for both of us. It was only Netty who held me together with her uniqueness and tremendous love. Only now was I beginning to see the talent and ability and stamina of the woman. She has fantastic talent. She has tremendous hands that do creative things and cook, my God, can she cook! Her warmth and strength is incredible and it is no surprise at all that the poor loved her.

She was never really scared either — for Willie or for herself. Willie became an instant friend of everyone who came. People would have us believe that we should be afraid of the poor, afraid of child molesters, etc. But this is the myth, the propaganda we have been filled with about the poor — how we must fear them.

Certainly there are isolated examples such as the one I related earlier, but society has made us fear the poor. That way one can more easily rationalize as to why he does nothing to help the beggar.

The diabolical way whites have been taught to fear the blacks ("Lock your car doors when you drive through the black sections!") is all part of the same thing. The skid row men are made out to be dangerous, to be dirty old men. This simply is not true. As these people would come into our home, we would find them very ordinary people. They were economically poor, sometimes without much education, but really brothers and sisters of our Willie in our little community.

Willie is a real product of that environment. We did try to operate the house in a certain rhythm and to create the kind of womb a child can really grow up in. Often things grew chaotic, but the life was harder on us than it was on Willie.

Of course, I gave all the credit for that to Netty — an incredibly fine mother. Her own environment in northern Wisconsin and her strong father had prepared her well for what what she was doing. She lived a hard life, but she had always worked hard. On the farm she had gotten up early to milk the cows. She was never afraid of work.

Being a nurse was natural to her. It fit her whole personality. It certainly prepared her to be a great mother. In the confusion of that house and in the second Casa Maria, the children were never lacking the attention and care they needed. As a matter of fact, I think our children are advanced precisely because of the hospitality house and I think the larger community situation there made them more alert and less afraid than had they been reared just by the two of us.

And so, the poor became a real part of our lives, a real part of our family. I am not saying that I, or Netty, for that matter, completely identified with the poor. Again, the difference between ourselves and the real poor was that our poverty was voluntary. I knew I could make it. I could always make a living out there. Many of the poor are not able to do that, not just because of society or their environment, but because of the physical condition and mental capacity of their own lives.

Neither am I saying that serving the poor is a romantic, pleasant, happy job. In one sense, of course, the poor are very interesting people — mostly because they are people. They are not as simple as most other people like to think them to be. Mostly they are like you and me. They are a product of society. They read the same papers and accept the same media. They listen to a lot of radio and watch a lot of TV. They are programmed just like the rest of us.

They are materialists and hunger after what television says will make them happy. They have not chosen to be free of material possessions.

Generally, they are the best buyers of the system, the most sold on America, the best believers of the American dream, the most defensive of the establishment. If you talk about creating great solutions to their social ills and needs, they will fight you. All one can do is become their brother — that they understand.

Among themselves, they have the same fears and hatreds, the same need to be better than someone else, the same racism as the rest of society. How could we expect otherwise? Why should we expect the unprivileged, uneducated poor to be humanitarian? Men who deal daily on the most basic level of survival have little concern for their brothers. They, too, have been taught the American ideal of competition. There is competition, even greater competition, in the lowest levels of our society. The men on Skid Row are in competition with one another. Each man has his own hustle. They cut one another's throats, they roll one another in the streets.

That is why Casa Maria confronted them so. It was an utter contradiction to their own life-styles. They had never been totally accepted before, without filling in any forms, without any questions about their background — and without even hearing a sermon or being asked to convert or change.

We felt it was not up to us to judge anyone who came to join our family. No matter how long a man's been on Skid Row, no matter if he's divorced, no matter if he's left his family, no matter if he's a murderer, no matter if he's a soldier or a war victim — the place to stand is to respect that man and treat him as your brother. You respect the man's humanness. Humanity is the real value. And you respect him for his uniqueness, his distinct gifts, his peculiar abilities. Some of the poor, of course, have fantastic backgrounds — in business, education, etc.

All the while, I knew I had the ability and certainly the confidence in myself to go out and make money and be successful — if that's what being successful means. But gradually, imperceptibly, I was beginning to lose the freedom to choose to do that. I began to realize I was hooked, and Netty was hooked along with me, in her own right and in her own way.

I began to see that psychologically I was trapped — for the rest of my life. I had seen too much, I had watched too much. I had grown too close to the situation of the poor ever to return to comfortable middle-class society. In some way, in some form, I was committed to building some new society, somewhere, wherever and whenever possible.

Nevertheless, the daily demands were sometimes too much. Though young and energetic, though ideologically sure what I was doing was right and necessary, I saw that if I were going to be effective in the community of Casa Maria, if I was really going to build and mold a future for my children and for my society, I had to look outside the walls of Casa and see what was happening there.

I looked — long and hard, and what I saw didn't make sense to me. I asked a lot of questions and got no answers. I began to wonder if I was being called to the larger community to challenge the priorities of a great nation gone mad.

CHAPTER SIX

That first Casa Maria on the south side could have continued on and on. No one really came down on us, not even the law. Although many people did not understand and some people thought we were encouraging drop-outs and bums, most people recognized the good that we were doing. There really was little they could criticize.

To those who knew him, Mike Cullen was a nice guy, a friendly guy, a good Irishman, and what he and his wife were doing was a real Christian thing. And so Netty (with Brennan) and Willie and I continued to live in our one room (we did have a closet) and to do what nice people thought was a nice thing to do.

But I guess Netty and I knew down deep that we could not continue on this way for very long. Once we opened our lives completely, we had to be open to the pressing needs and problems of the whole community — not just to those immediately surrounding us. We began to feel the need to speak to the larger questions of the larger community. We began to see our work in relation to what was happening to the country and to the world. It became impossible to ignore the environment, the conditions which caused or at least brought on the inhuman and sub-human status of the poor.

As I stated earlier, I began to ask questions. Even though I had walked in the Groppi demonstrations and was somewhat involved in the civil rights movement, for the most part I was withdrawn. I could hardly be called a protestor or a radical.

But now a new beginning was happening. My whole consciousness was beginning to change. And more and more my thoughts began to focus on the horror of killing — any kind of killing, and particularly on the killing our government was perpetuating by means of billions of tax dollars, the killing of our brothers and sisters in Vietnam.

Daily I was struggling to preserve life. Daily Casa Maria was scrounging for anything and everything just to keep body and soul together. How could it be that the poor, the dispossessed of this country had to beg to stay alive and that we at Casa were devoting our whole lives to keeping people alive when our government was spending billions to kill and perverting and destroying our young men by forcing them to kill — and to be killed?

It didn't make any sense. I didn't understand — and the poor I talked to didn't understand, and most people I met didn't understand.

Why were our priorities so bad? Why were our cities burning? Why were our cities rotting? Why were our poor so visible in this, the richest nation in the world?

Because of my rearing, my education, my entire formation, I turned to the Church. My faith demanded that the Church speak out on these matters, that Catholics be heard concerning these most important issues which were at the core of the Gospels, the heart and soul of Christianity.

Pope Paul had come to the United Nations pleading for peace. "War — never again." This same Paul had written the fantastic document, "Progressio Populorum," which deals with the equal distribution of the goods of the earth. Pope Paul had written that the goods of the earth belong to all the people.

But he, like the rest of the Church, lost credibility. Though truly a man of peace, he did not press for peace in any real and compelling way.

Besides, Paul had become incredible with his naive and simplistic approach to birth control, by not listening to his own commission. He also became incredible by his absurd trips to Latin America and to Africa, where he traveled and acted more like a Johnson, a Nixon, or an Agnew, a man of state rather than a man of God.

Yet, I do not blame the man personally. He, too, is formed by his culture, his background. He is a diplomat, not a revolutionary. The world deserves a Pope John only once every several centuries.

Pope Paul is thoroughly, totally a son, a product of the Church. Like millions of others, I began to see the institutional Church as just another corporation, dedicated to self-interest, self-preservation, self-perpetuation. All of these goals are natural and un-Christian. Much, if not all, of the institutional Church cannot even be Christian, the Church of Christ. The Church corporation cannot live the message of Christ — that unless the grain of wheat dies, it cannot bear fruit. The Church corporation never really gets down to the message — the simple message of the Gospel.

94

Never has that been more true than in the Church's general silence about war, about the possession of nuclear weapons, about the heinous and monstrous killing of our brothers and sisters in Vietnam.

I began to see the Church, not as a sign of hope and of life, but as a silent approver of death and destruction. Of course, in a sense, the Church has always been that — ever since the Church shook hands with Constantine. The Crusades were a bad joke, the religious wars were insane, the silence of the Church in Hitler's Germany was inexcusable, the rejoicing of the Church over Hiroshima and Nagasaki was almost masochistic (both were very Catholic areas). And so, I guess we could not be surprised by the silence of American bishops, American Catholics, about what Catholics and other Americans were doing in Vietnam.

Somehow the early Christians had the courage to say no to killing and destruction, perhaps because the message of Christ was so fresh in their lives. Perhaps that is why they were willing to be led to the slaughterhouse and to be eaten up by lions rather than compromise. But the Constantine people began to water down the message and to wallow in compromise.

But the Church will survive. She is bigger than all of us and stands over history and popes and bishops and time and circumstances.

And what's so fantastic about the Church as corporation is that, unlike other corporations, she has a built-in revolution inside her. As corporation she has a way of destroying herself — especially when she gets too big. Maybe that's God's mystery. The Church as corporation is destroying herself. The Church as corporation is literally being destroyed in and of itself. She is not being destroyed by the state. On the contrary, in most instances the state would like to keep her the way she is.

Vatican II served to show us that the corporation is not where it's at. It was difficult for many who had believed in and served that corporation for thirty, forty, or more years to watch it break up, to see that it was no longer a sign of what they thought it was supposed to be. People, priests, nuns and lay people, suddenly realized that they were being crippled and stifled by the legalisms of the corporation which had nothing to do with Christ or with Christianity.

I began to see that only if this corporation continues to crumble can the real Church, the real Kingdom of heaven be reborn. The fact that this is happening then is no reason for despair or loss of faith. On the contrary, it is the occasion for hope and rejoicing. I felt and still feel as if my faith is much stronger than ever before. More than ever, I understand why I have the faith. The institution is not and will not prevent me from being a Christian. Christ did not establish a corporation, but he initiated the Kingdom of Heaven, and that is mostly a lived-out attitude of mind. And you know that the faith is a mystery and a gift and there's no real way of defining it.

These are the thoughts I began to have about the Church as I began looking outside the walls of Casa Maria and all that the people of Casa Maria were teaching me. The Church was a part of me and I knew I would never leave her, but I also knew I had to be honest and that the Spirit was not tied to one man or merely to the hierarchy.

At this time we were celebrating Mass as often as we could at Casa. Priests who were moving into new things, into new directions, were stopping in and we were celebrating what at that time were considered "radical" Masses. Some people were shocked and went home and called the chancery (the archdiocesan officials, the archbishop's boys) and so we were getting the evil eye of the "officiales."

One poor priest almost got expelled from the priesthood for offering one of those radical Masses. He used ordinary bread, for example, and everybody drank from the cup, and I usually read the epistle and kind of led the people in prayers and songs.

We simply felt that this is the way Christ would have done things. We felt close to the Spirit of the Last Supper, and, of course, again, most of what we did then which was so far out is now commonplace and even accepted by many dioceses throughout the world.

As Lent came in that spring of 1967, I thought of doing what Christians for centuries had done during Lent. I decided I must fast.

But my fast had to be a sign. It had to deal with the real and the concrete. My fast had to speak to the community, to the world. My fast would be in protest of the continued waste of lives and money in a senseless war.

But where and how would I do this? I decided to speak to the faith-community, that community I believed in and was such a part of all my life. I decided to go to the "seat" of the faith in Milwaukee. I went to the cathedral to fast for one week, from Palm Sunday to Easter Sunday.

(So I went to St. John's Cathedral on the day after Palm Sunday in March of 1967 to speak with my life on an eight-day fast. I undertook the fast mainly because I came out of a Christian heritage of fasting. I wasn't at this time a follower of Gandhi. I had never read the life of Mahatma Gandhi. I read a little of Martin King in terms of his life and his work, but I never read a great amount of Mahatma Gandhi up to this time. I had never read a book on Vietnam. I only knew what I saw in the paper and on the news media. But I knew we were spending billions on a war that was robbing us, robbing society of the money needed at home to rebuild our cities and to supply the needs of the poor.

And so I found myself at St. John's Cathedral fasting and it was quite an overwhelming experience. To my amazement, it achieved much more notoriety in the media than I ever expected. I had a statement which I presented to Monsignor Kelly, the rector of the cathedral, and I told him I was going to be in the cathedral for six to seven days, and I hoped I would not cause any trouble or inconvenience to him. I told him I intended to stay day and night, and intended to fast. Monsignor Kelly, a good, gentle man, was very responsive and he said okay. He faced a little bit of trouble from parishioners who called and expressed their outrage that this young man was staging his protest in the cathedral. After all, it was a catherdal! I don't blame those people either. All the circumstances of their lives lead them to think in this way.

Frankly, I was scared! I had spoken to Monsignor Kelly after the eight o'clock Mass which I had attended. Mike McCann brought me a big overcoat that morning and Barbara Schmoll of "The Milwaukee Journal" was there. I gave her a copy of my statement and she wrote about what I was doing for the Journal.

Perhaps the most significant aspect of the entire experience was the amount of publicity given to it. I was amazed that people would at all be interested, that they would think this was important. Here I was, just one person fasting and it came off as if there had been a huge demonstration.

I did more than just sit and fast. I prayed a lot and I read a lot of Scripture, both from the Old Testament and the New. I also read two books during that week. One was the life of Mahatma Gandhi and the other was *Vietnam: Lotus in a Sea of Fire* by Thich Nhat Hanh, a Buddhist pacifist, who was sensitive to the life and death of Vietnamese and Americans and saw the tragedy of what was happening in his country. His book touched me deeply because I could see he was speaking from the depth of his own being, and not just as a Vietnamese whose country had been invaded by someone from outside the borders. He was speaking as a man, a Buddhist, a man sensitive to life, and I could relate to that. The book had a deep impact upon my life.

Also, Mahatma Gandhi opened up a whole new array of things for me. He showed me there was a new way, there was a way that we could bring about social change. It was radical in the sense that in its essence it was tied to man and woman, to the very being of men and women. Gandhi spent a lifetime seeking the truth. He taught me that to seek the truth is to speak what is right. His life made such an impact that I knew I could never go back to living differently than the way I was living at that time. I knew that as long as there are poor people in society it is our responsibility to stand at their side.)

97

In just a day or so I began receiving letters. I met so many beautiful people. One woman came to me in the cathedral and very silently, without saying a word, handed me a sign of spring — some pussywillows.

Another man, a Jewish business man, came and spent part of a day with me. He said he didn't understand what I was doing or why, but that if I was doing it, it had to be important.

A Lutheran minister and his family came to visit me. A rabbi came, and many students, many who had never been in any protest before. All of this just blew my mind.

It told me that a new kind of community was beginning to happen. It told me that what I was doing was so terribly correct, that what I was doing was such an obvious expression of life. I had no way of knowing the full implications my saying no could have.

On Good Friday I decided to march for peace. I carried a huge crucifix and walked about six miles from twelve to three in the afternoon down to the south side of Milwaukee. I couldn't believe it — thirty people marched with me. One of them was Father Dismas Becker, O.C.D., who was in the beginning of his involvement with the poor on the Milwaukee scene. Two of the people walking with us were Communists. This was so new to me because I had been born and raised with a tremendous fear and hatred of Communists. But they walked with me and that was beautiful, that was important, and I began to have a new attitude about certain political ideologies.

We walked all the way to Our Lady Queen of Peace Church that day. I felt that a church with that name would be a good place to pray for peace.

I was afraid we would have a hassle of some kind at the church. I had also grown a beard that Lent — not particularly to prove anything, but because I felt free enough to do it. Yet, I was very conscious of it — even fearful of it. I didn't want to be identified as a hippie, or even as a peacenik. I was too proud, much too proud. I couldn't wait for Lent to end to shave it off. I felt wearing it was a real penance because I wanted to be accepted and not looked down upon.

Anyway, we arrived at the church just as Holy Communion was being distributed. I approached the monsignor who was giving out Communion and when he saw me, he set the ciborium (the container holding the Communion wafers or hosts) down and embraced me. Before all those people! And he said, "You are welcome here." I really cried — I just couldn't believe it.

Even at the cathedral there had been talk of having me thrown out. One usher called the police the first night I was there. But we stayed there at Our Lady Queen of Peace on the "conservative south side" and prayed. After the regular Good Friday services we held a kind of liturgy for peace. Then we went back to the cathedral.

I stayed there until Easter Sunday after the archbishop's Mass and then I returned to Casa Maria.

But I returned a different man. My life had taken a drastic new turn. In one short week I found myself on the front lines.

The media had turned my life around and thereafter I and the whole of Casa Maria were known, not as the servants of the poor, but as peaceniks. Suddenly Casa Maria had a bad name. Working for the poor was fine, but working for peace was political. Suddenly Mike Cullen and Casa Maria were political and all the machinery of the system — the system that did not want to acknowledge that working for the poor and working for peace were one and the same, that the two cannot be separated — came grinding down upon us and we knew that it would not be content until Casa Maria was ground into extinction.

It was hard to say where the pressures were coming from because the system is capable of doing things very sophisticatedly, of making its actions seem decent and right.

For the first time we began seeing a guy from the health department. For the first time we were told that we were violating all kinds of laws.

And the Church, the contented concubine of the state, must have had tremendous pressure put on her because suddenly we were told that Casa Maria had to be governed strictly by an acting Board of Directors. Our building, of course, belonged to the diocese and they were paying some of the utilities, etc., and now there had to be a strict accounting for all the money that was being spent.

The Board of Directors that we did have consisted of about ten people — some very big and important names in the Milwaukee community. It was these people, most of them, who were most upset by my "political" action of demonstrating for peace. Some of them immediately wanted to withdraw from the scene completely.

(A lot of the pressure that came on our lives from people outside our immediate community was from people who didn't understand what we were doing, who were caught up in a kind of false patriotism, people who felt that in order to be a patriot in this country, they must support anything the country does, and particularly, whatever the military does. This is part of the tragedy of our nation. We have some 25,000,000 veterans and that in essence gives us the basis for being a military state. Veterans, and through them, millions of other Americans, are brainwashed into look- ing to the military to find all the solutions to the problems that divide mankind. History has tried to teach us that military means cannot be a solution to anybody's problems, including political problems at home and abroad. This is particularly true for large nations, be they Russia or U.S. or China, who have the power to annihilate the human family. Military solutions cannot work, and so we are all made poor. Nuclear weapons have made us all poor, whether economically rich or poor. We are all left trembling in fear, for when these weapons are used, those who used them will have also perished. By a strange paradox, the military might of our times has once and for all put rich and poor nations in the same helpless plight. If we are to survive at all, we are compelled to build a world community without war, without the military.

When we defend our freedom, when we pretend to defend democracy with the barrel of a gun, we are losing it. Never has that been more true than today. What is said of the U.S. is also true of Russia. Russia is helpless before the demands of Czechoslovakia. All small countries, every country must be able to form its own destiny and large countries have a tremendous responsibility to grant freedom to every nation.

All this became quite clear, when I returned to Casa after my fast. When I got back, it was so evident that people did not understand. They told me I was unpatriotic. They said, Mike Cullen, it's nice that you feed our poor, but you don't have the right to speak about our country's ills. After all you're not even a citizen.

These people had forgotten that their grandfathers and grandmothers had come out of the same sod and the same soil and the same part of the world that I had come out of, though I came a few generations later.

These people had forgotten what America used to be — for all peoples. It was a land of opportunity. It was almost like the Promised Land sought by the people of Israel. The Hebrews knew they could build a new society, the new Jerusalem.

But the majority of Americans are trapped. We have been betrayed by one another. We have become profit-seekers rather than seekers of the common good. And so the American dream is nullified. But the weight lies on all of us, not just on Americans, but on Vietnamese, Chinese, Latin Americans, Africans and Europeans. We must all understand that we are now a global village and no longer totally separate nations. We are all one people, a common people, all of us, and that's the future of the world — if we are to have one, and only then can we explore the planets and what have you. Otherwise I think we are going to annihilate ourselves, and I don't say that by way of platitude. I think it's true. I believe it is exactly true. I don't think it's abstract. I think it's fact.)

So this is June of 1967. About May, Netty and I realized there was no way of going on at the location of the first Casa Maria. The pressures from the diocese were too great there and it was very obvious that the diocese wasn't going to provide us with a new house.

Then one day someone called me up and said there was a house over on North 21st Street, big as a barn. We could rent it practically for nothing or we could buy it.

It was a huge, monstrous barn for sure and the place certainly needed painting. The house had been vacant for more than nine months. The walls were all cracked and it bore the scars of typical vandalism.

The whole block there on 21st Street was a bare and desolate kind of place, a kind of ghost town. It is important to relate this because after Casa Maria grew to a community of several houses, people in the near-by neighborhood and certain politicians claimed that we had lowered the value of the property in our neighborhood. This charge became stronger after my involvement with the Milwaukee 14. Actually, the opposite is true. Property value went up after we lived there for a while.

(Let me tell you a little bit about what I saw in the neighborhood when we came. It was a very poor neighborhood. The houses were in bad shape. You could see they were a grand part of the city at one time, but they had been abandoned. They had been abandoned by people who didn't want to live in that neighborhood any more, who were afraid of the change, afraid of what they call the changing neighborhood, of the influx of the poor. Many of these poor were from the South who were moving or had moved to the North because they could no longer live on the income that they were making in the deep South. So they were trying to find work in the urban areas of the northern part of this country. In the past, many Europeans did the same thing. They came in and lived in certain sections of the city. But now it was the black people of the South and the poor people of the Southwest, the migrant workers, Spanish workers, Mexican workers, Puerto Rican workers, who had become part of this society and had come to get jobs in the cities of northern U.S.

So the white community that liked its own neighborhood wasn't able to live with these new kinds of people, these people who lived differently or who acted or looked differently. So they fled the central city and began to develop suburban communities and we found this neighborhood abandoned like a ghost town, from Juneau to Highland. People with credentials, people with educational backgrounds, people who could begin to benefit the neighborhood had moved out. The housing one block east of us was a project called K-3 where thousands of homes have been taken down in the recent years. It's what I always refer to as our Hanoi in Milwaukee, the central city of Milwaukee. The city has torn down more homes than it has replaced, and, of course, this area is still a wasteland at this late hour, where the poor used to live and where even more poor are homeless as a result of that property being torn down and nothing built in its place. We knew our neighborhood was the next one, only one block away, so we thought buying into that neighborhood would be important.)

101

The "new" house was most important to me because of Netty. I loved her so much and do love her so much that I had to know she was in a house and a location where she could function in a more human way. She had no retreat in the old house and sometimes things would get so hectic that she thought her nerves were going to break. Anybody could see that the conditions of the house did make this a real possibility, and God knows, I knew I could not make it without Netty. She had become so much a part of me, so much . . .

When Netty looked at the big house, she immediately loved it, especially the woodwork — or perhaps I should say, at least the woodwork. I was so excited because she liked it, all I could say was wow, we're going to get it. Come hell or high water we're going to get it.

I hadn't been working for some months and we just didn't have any money. But about six months after we had opened the first Casa Maria, Netty and I had gone to New York City to visit Dorothy Day. It was quite an experience. So at this time I wrote to Dorothy and asked if she would come to Milwaukee to give a talk or something to raise money for us.

Well, Dorothy wrote back and all she said was, Michael, Michael, where is your faith? You must pray — and God will provide a house. Did this blow my mind! And, of course, I knew she was right. I knew she was right.

But I had written to Father Dan Berrigan, too. I had met Dan in Milwaukee, about the same time I first met Dorothy in New York. He had come to Milwaukee and had given a talk somewhere on the south side. I believe this was shortly after being exiled by his Jesuit superiors to South America.

After Dan's talk I stood up to ask some questions about the war. I told him about Casa Maria and invited him to stay with us. Of course he came. Of all the places the brilliant priest-poet could have stayed in Milwaukee, of course he chose to stay with the poor at Casa Maria.

I met Dan again at Rosary College some time later. Corita Kent, the great artist-serigrapher, at that time still an Immaculate Heart of Mary nun, was also at Rosary. We became good friends with Corita, too, and she gave us a number of original silk screenings to raffle off to raise money for the house.

Anyway, after our second meeting, Dan Berrigan and I began to correspond from time to time, and so, at the same time I wrote to Dorothy Day, I wrote to Dan, asking him to come and perform some kind of benefit for us.

Dan said he would come and we arranged to have him speak at the Marquette University High School auditorium. We raised about $1,000.00 and that became the down payment for the new Casa Maria.

So we began to move to the big house on 21st Street. We took everything along that we had collected on the south side. The Commandos, Father Groppi's gang, did most of the moving.

The move did not change the nature of our work. We continued to serve the poor, to shelter the homeless. But because the new house needed so much work, we had to find a place for many of the people who had been with us regularly at the other house. Some of these people were seriously mentally sick, and we simply had to find other help for them.

The big task immediately before us was to get the house in shape. The first thing we did was to beg fifty gallons of red barn paint. Actually, the paint was a darker red than usual barn paint, and I suppose that's why the paint hadn't sold. But it was plenty good for us.

We didn't even have a ladder. We went out and rented a spray gun and that big old house began soaking up paint. It hadn't been painted for some sixteen years and I don't know how many gallons we sprayed on her.

We also started immediately to do some paneling inside the house. I was becoming more of a carpenter every day, and I thought of those days in my youth when I wanted to become a carpenter as a lay brother missionary in Africa.

But we had a lot of trouble getting a hold on the house. We were trying to buy it, of course, but we were also trying to obtain a mortgage. I had already put a lot of work and money into the house, but the final buying of it was a real pain.

The main reason was that the house belonged to what I considered a typical slumlord, although in this case the slumlord was some kind of corporation. They were money-grabbers just the same.

Eventually we won — but only because of the generous and professional efforts of E. Michael McCann. We desperately needed him and he came through beautifully.

I realized, too, that I had to get a job. Someone called me and told me this job was available at the Wisconsin State Employment Service as some kind of community specialist. So I said to myself, why not? But this was a Civil Service job and one has to be a U.S. citizen for a Civil Service job. I wasn't much into the war protest at this time and resentment to my earlier actions had simmered down quite a bit. But I was amazed that I got the job. I was happy to get it.

The work fit in with my whole vocation. I was to teach very illiterate and poor people the skills of getting a job. As usual for me, the opportunity was a great learning experience for me. Most of the people I dealt with were black, as were most of the teachers. I learned a lot of black history and taught a lot of black history, and I really began to see the need for black pride.

But I also learned a lot about the games employers play, how they interview people and the false situations they create. I taught people how to take tests and employment exams and showed the poor what they were like and how to pass them. But I saw the injustice, the hypocrisy of many employers who externally were acting as if they were fair in seeking the best qualified person for a job. Why was it that black people were expected to apply for the janitor's job?

I had this job for almost a year and really enjoyed it and benefitted from it. Our "course" was about two weeks long. We had about forty students at a time and as many as a thousand blacks must have gone through that program while I was there.

Obviously, we did other kinds of teaching, too. Even though some blacks wondered why that "white dude" was hanging around, most of them recognized me as a soul brother. I didn't care if I was working for the state, the job didn't tie me down or limit me. The real action was out on the streets at night and every night I was out there walking and many of my students with me.

After the two-week course we always had "graduation" parties. These were really something — real "soul" parties, with dancing and singing. I think I really got into the black culture thing and as usual, I was wildly enthusiastic.

The job worked hand in hand with much of what Casa Maria was all about. Many of the people who came to Casa for a place to stay I was able to bring down for employment training. The life-style Netty and I had was what made me credible to those in need of help. They believed me when I said I would help — whether that was to get a job or something else.

But the real star at this time was Netty. During the day I was away for at least eight hours and it was Netty who ran the show. At this time we became real partners and I fully realized Casa could not stay open a day without Netty. We complemented each other perfectly. The work was hard, very hard, and the demands on Netty were incredible. But, then, she is an incredible woman.

I began to see her take a real leadership position. She made decisions and she made them well. Heaven knows ours was not an ordinary house. It was a center for all kinds of activities. Visitors from all over the U.S. and elsewhere were constantly popping in. There were speeches and discussions and meetings held there constantly. But Netty endured and grew — and in between it all gave birth to Brennan and she was a terrific mother to both Willie and the new baby.

I can't dwell on Netty long. She's very difficult to talk about. She has meant so much to me. It has never been just a matter of loving

104

her. She's in my bones, my veins, my head, my spirit. She's everything of me and I am everything of her. We are really married.

I say this in spite of the obvious fact that we sometimes had real battles. Most often the conflicts were merely a matter of misunderstanding and not of having enough time to talk. There were times that I really thought the whole thing was going to break up. But even though it was harder on me than on her it was she who kept us together. She stuck by me in those incredible times — and later, when I'm sure she didn't understand what the hell I was doing.

Netty would tell herself that she knew when we met and when she married me that she would never live an ordinary life. She knew she was marrying more than me. She knew she would at some time live a life that would be unsettling and very difficult. Netty had that insight. She saw and understood what I really didn't see myself. In other words, she knew me better than I knew myself. I used to talk about being a deacon, of the possibility of the Church allowing married deacons. She knew I would want that, that the Church also was a part of my bones and that I wanted to live the full life of the Church.

(So we went on, as best we knew how, feeding the hungry, providing shelter, giving clothes to the cold, filling food baskets, getting people to clinics and hospitals who wouldn't and often couldn't get there, getting medical care, getting welfare, teaching them to know their rights, getting jobs.

And Casa Maria began to expand. One of our people, Father Larry Rosebaugh, later one of the Milwaukee 14, opened up a place called the Living Room on State Street. Here they began to take in men off the street, men whom polite society would label Skid Row men. The Living Room lifted a tremendous burden off our shoulders and enabled us to deal more with families.

As I began to speak about the war, people began to think I was more concerned with peace than I was concerned with the poor. But being concerned with the poor is the heart of peace-making. If we can't respond to our brothers on a personal level, we really don't have anything to say about the Vietnamese war or war anywhere because it is there you touch Vietnam most deeply, it's there you preach the best sermon about peace.

But there were a lot of young people who didn't know their rights about the draft and we found ourselves doing some draft counselling. We often spent more time with the young than we were able to spend with the poor because the young didn't know they had rights, that they had alternatives under the law. There weren't enough lawyers working on behalf of young men who wanted to see what their rights are.

105

Many young people got to know us because of my work for peace. I had also demonstrated my resistance that year. I burned my draft card and I did it not as an outrage against any person, but to show people symbolically that I could no longer see the military as a solution to problems on a global scale. We had to begin to renounce war as a way to the future and the way I could renounce it was to burn my draft card. I did it in a Catholic Church. I wasn't confronting any person or government. I was simply saying no, that I could no longer in conscience as a person continue without saying no as best I knew how at that time. That was done some time in March of 1968, and I knew it would bring my life into jeopardy because it had apparently had a legal penalty attached to it. I knew I could be arrested at any time, but I took on that responsibility, I took on that risk.

Later on, of course, I found myself advising young men to do likewise if their conscience so dictated. But it had to be their conscience that was doing it, not mine.

People must resist evil as best they know how, but hopefully in a human fashion, in a human way. We must stay human, because that is the important part of where we are in history. Perhaps some should resist taxes, taxes which are going to make war. Some eighty per cent of our tax dollar goes to the military. Do men and women have the courage to stop paying the war machine? These are tough questions, but they can be answered only by you and me, and with the fullness of our humanity, staying alive and staying human. That's the heart of the thing.

So I found myself talking to more and more people, young and old, about peace. But our work for the poor continued as the most important thing.

By late fall of 1968, we had a chance to take over an old church right across the street from Casa Maria, the Highland Methodist Church, which no longer was used as a church, because it no longer had a congregation. So we asked the Methodist Church, though I am a Roman Catholic, because I felt it was also an opportunity for ecumenism. We were all Christians who hold the same Gospel, the same value system, though we may differ theologically. We could work together by feeding the hungry. The Methodists responded very generously and offered to pay the heat and electricity of the basement of the church.

So we started feeding more men and it took the burden away from the house. We could now be a little more human than we had been in the two previous years. The program there, called The Meal, began to feed some one hundred men daily. We did this for nearly a year before that church was taken away from us because the city decided the building was no longer a church, but a social center and therefore it had to be re-classified and then the building had to be closed because of zoning laws. Incredible!

But now we are over at St. Michael's church, four or five blocks away from our immediate neighborhood, feeding the same men. It's a little more inconvenient for the men on State Street who need our help, but the hungry are being fed.)

During this time our publication, "The Catholic Radical" was increasing in size, quality, and distribution. We had started out at the old Casa Maria with a newsletter called, "The Casa Maria Cry." But the paper developed and soon we had it printed. Way back, Dorothy Day was going to call her paper "The Catholic Radical," but to counter-act the Communist paper, "The Daily Worker," she called her paper, which is still published and sold for a penny a copy, "The Catholic Worker."

"The Catholic Radical," again, radical meaning getting back to the roots, gave us a wider voice and Casa Maria became even better known. At times, of course, this meant more support and at other times, more criticism and condemnation.

Other things were also happening. One of our people started a bookstore called "Rhubarb," and it became the center for the selling of radical books, of publications dealing with the Third World, etc.

Other groups of people began to move into our 21st Street block — people of various ideologies, some religious, some Maoist, some merely experimenting in communal living at various levels. Casa Maria was no longer Mike and Netty Cullen, but a community of people with differing backgrounds. A group of young Jesuits lived in one house, and Father Norm Frederick, a Milwaukee diocesan priest, became a real and indispensable part of our household and of "The Catholic Radical."

Also, as Willie got older, Netty and I realized that we didn't want him in one of our neighborhood jails that were supposed to be schools. They were jails in every sense of the word, with fierce regimentation and insensitive teachers.

So we began developing an alternative. We began trying to develop a pre-school Montessori school. We acquired some excellent voluntary teachers, and a real start was made.

All these things were beginning to happen — and in such a short time. Who knows how far they would have gone? Who knows what Casa Maria would have become?

But things began to move in other directions. A series of events and personalities began to turn my head into a direction which would be even a greater trial for Netty and the children.

One such personality was Father Daniel Berrigan. I began to know Dan, not as an intellectual or as a poet (and heaven knows he is both), but as a friend. Dan became the guy I could completely open my mind to.

Dan was and is a man of the Gospels, a man who loves the Gospel, a man who loves the message of Jesus. He's truly a Christian. He is a man of the Church, despite the inadequacies. He is very critical of the institutional Church, but his unique faith goes much deeper than any institution or any corporation.

Dan became a real source of strength. I was strengthened by his honesty. He was a priest and he was saying the things he knew he had to say, in spite of any consequences from the Church or the State. The bishops were not speaking out on the important issues and so Dan Berrigan was becoming our bishop.

A young man by the name of Bill Taylor stayed with us for a while at Casa. Bill was from California and he had heard Dan speak at Immaculate Heart College. When Bill heard that Dan was giving a retreat out in Boston, he took off for Boston. The retreat turned out to be a three-day conference on the war. Dan was basing his stand against killing, against war, on the Scriptures. Dan was saying that the Christian obviously had to say no to war. Bill Taylor had taped Dan's talks and when he returned to Casa, we listened to the tapes over and over — especially on Friday evenings, when, Catholic Worker style, we used to have roundtable discussions.

Through these tapes and from other visits and visitors, the war became a real concern of ours. We began to discuss non-violence and what it had to mean in our lives. People like Caesar Chavez came to stay with us. We were overwhelmed by his holiness, his gentleness, his humanity, and he spoke of non-violence.

As I mentioned earlier, I had visited Dan and he had visited Casa. His very being, his dress, his living quarters, everything about him exemplified voluntary poverty. He usually dressed in a simple light jacket and wore a turtle-neck shirt or sweater. He traveled light. He never carried a suitcase but had only a couple of books in a bag under his arm.

Dan lived in one room — his bathroom, his desk, his bed, his books — everything was in one room. He never locked his door. His room was in a public apartment building and anyone could come and steal anything he had.

His walls were full of paintings and pictures. The pictures were mostly of his heroes like Thomas Merton, Martin King, Mahatma Gandhi. His bathroom was full of poems. He even showered with poems. The man is pure artist — everything plain and simple but in excellent taste.

He had a cross that was burned at Selma and another cross burned by the KKK.

It was Dan, who impressed me, overwhelmed me by his person and his style, who tied poverty and the war together for me. It was through Dan, of course, that I met his brother, Father Phil Berrigan. Phil was not a Jesuit but a Josephite, and he, too, blew my mind.

I met Phil for the first time on the march on the Pentagon in October of 1967. I asked him to come to Milwaukee and he did. He spent a very quiet week with us and never even hinted to us that he would be pouring blood over some draft files in Baltimore just a couple of weeks later.

This act of Phil's really had an effect on me. Fantastic! I had no trouble with it at all. Phil came to Milwaukee after that and spoke at Marquette. There was a counter demonstration, and for the first time I became aware of police taking pictures of us. I was beginning to be a hunted person — one of those radicals.

Phil impressed me as the perfect complement of Dan. While Dan is thin and frail, Phil is huge and strong. Dan is the intellectual, the poet. Phil is much more practical. Phil had been in the civil rights movement for years, and was afraid of nothing.

Dan had gotten himself arrested for refusing to leave the Pentagon after that October march. Dan was spending his first days in jail when Phil and a couple of others poured the blood.

Phil's practical, political mind influenced all of us. He knew things like how much the government spends per year on weapons and materials for war. He knew how many troops the U.S. had and where they were. He told us how much of every tax dollar went for destruction. Phil knew well how our cities were rotting, how much housing was needed.

Phil told us that the obvious thing the Christian had to do was to say no. And we had to say no loudly enough for everyone to hear. As Christians we had to say no non-violently.

The pouring of blood exemplified everything Phil was talking about. It was all very simple and very clear. And what was also very clear was that the Baltimore act was invitational.

Then rumors started coming from the East, rumors of invitations to some action. No invitation came to me, but I knew something was up. There definitely was an action in the making.

We didn't know what it was all about, but all of a sudden on the news one night we learned of the burning of draft files by homemade napalm. This time Dan was with Phil, and there were seven others who made up the Catonsville Nine. Someone from Baltimore sent us a special delivery letter with all the news and with the names of all the people involved.

I almost went out of my mind. My God! The times were really serious! These men were giving their lives. They weren't playing games. What a fantastically creative way to say no!

The appeal, the invitation to me, personally, was compelling, overwhelming, demanding. I had to do something. I had to stand with these men.

The resistance movement was tremendously broadened by the action of these nine Catholics — all people with faith operating in their lives, who had now formed a community of risk.

Before these actions of pouring blood and napalming files, there were young people who were able to say no to the system, who were able to go to jail for the sake of their consciences. David Miller, for example, a Catholic Worker youth, who went out and gave a talk and burned his card publicly, bringing down the wrath and punishment of society and its system.

Now Dan and Phil and the others, people who were free, exempt from the draft and the war, had placed themselves in the same position as the young men who refused to pay homage to the system. These adults could have stayed clean and clear of the plight of the young, and like the upper and middle classes, live off the poor. The poor in this case were the young men who were stuck with their lot, subject to induction into an army and a war which they knew to be senseless and grossly immoral.

Along with this action, other events had made their mark on me and now everything came together to drive me to do something, to act, to scream my protest.

Martin King's death had shaken me to the depths of my being. I hadn't known him personally, but I had seen him and read him and my association with him went back to my seminary years.

I had gone to Resurrection City. Father Groppi and the Commandos were there and even without King, the event was momentous and imprinted itself deeply. It was a great coming together of the poor — the poor who for the first time saw themselves, not as black, not as white, not as Indian, not as Chicano, not as Puerto Rican, but as poor people — period. Obviously there were more black there, but the black began to see that poverty was not the same as black, that poverty was all colors. That was the greatest value of Resurrection City.

I lived there in a tent for three days. The poor experienced in Washington what they lived in their every-day lives — poverty in the fullest sense of the word. They lived it in those huts and in that mud. But there was a community operating there that they didn't have back home — and that's what they took back home with them, and that's what still affects this country, and that's why the Poor People's March was anything but a failure. Only shortsighted people without vision, who want immediate results, could call it a failure. People grow from experiment and experience. For me, the Poor People's March was just one more step along the way.

110

And then, Bobby Kennedy's death. I was visiting Daniel Berrigan at the time in Yonkers and we were up quite late when the phone rang. Someone told us to turn on our TV, that Bob Kennedy had been shot in Los Angeles. We just couldn't believe it. Dan had known the Kennedy family for a long time. He had offered Mass for Joseph and Rose in their Hyannisport home. But that was a couple of years before Dan became more and more politically involved.

We watched the television for a while and then, in the early dawn, we went out for a walk and some fresh air. We talked about Bobby. What if he had accepted the Gospel literally and sold everything and joined the Poor People's March? What would have happened to his political career? Where is the spiritual politician today? Why don't we have one Gandhi? Why don't we have men who are willing to serve the truth and not to compromise for the sake of income?

Another thing that influenced me deeply was the life of Franz Jagerstatter. I had read his life-story by Gordon Zahn, an American pacifist. Jagerstatter was a simple Austrian peasant with four children who resisted Hitler right from the beginning.

(From Hitler's entrance into Austria, Franz Jagerstatter said he would not stand by Hitler. When everybody used to say, "Heil, Hitler," this peasant, this uneducated man said, "Phooey, Hitler," and he stood alone for a long time. In February, 1943, Franz was inducted into the army, but he refused to obey orders right from the outset. He was placed in a stockade in Berlin and was executed six months later.

People tried to plead with him. Even priests and religious pleaded with him to retreat from his stand. But he knew better. He knew it was important for him to stand, to make a mark at that time — and he did.

Of course, I recognized Jagerstatter as a man of courage, a man who gives us faith today. He showed me that if we are to move out of our present state at this time in history, much deeper sacrifices would be demanded of the peace community. More was demanded than demonstrations and screaming and shouting and picketing and a lot of jargon. Personal sacrifice was demanded and deep sensitivity to one another.)

Carl Meyer, an associate editor of "The Catholic Worker," who lived in and ran St. Steven's Hospitality House in Chicago also confronted my life. He and his wife and two children spared nothing to serve the poor and to stand up for life — especially in his protests against capital punishment.

Then there was always Dorothy Day. When I went to see her, a woman some seventy-two years of age, I was amazed to find that she had as her roommate a woman with ulcerated, rotting legs, whom she had found in a New York subway. The stench was overwhelming as I entered her room. Here was Dorothy, still living what her whole life stood for — that a person's life is most valuable, and when life is destroyed on any level, part of us is destroyed.

The list of personalities and events that influenced me could go on and on. People like Father Tom Melville who was ejected from Guatemala for fostering revolution — revolution against the government our country was supporting with money and military hardware — came to Casa and touched my life.

All of these people were speaking to me out of the faith community that was so much a part of me.

It was especially, though, the action of the Catonsville 9, that provided the final push. I had to act.

CHAPTER SEVEN

When I learned the facts about the Catonsville 9, I simply had to take off. I left Casa Maria, alone. I had to think, I had to put things together. I had to act. The only question now was how? How could I stand alongside of those nine men? How could I register my protest? How could I put my life on the line for what I deeply believed?

I wandered about the country, hitchhiking much of the time. I went out East and got to talk to Dan and Phil and a few others. I began telling certain people I was planning an action in Milwaukee.

Dan was incredibly excited and alive. He was the center of attention in many people's minds, but there he was, back at his place of work, doing what he knew he had to do.

But his life had definitely taken on a new direction, a new dimension. He enjoyed what he had done and was very humorous about the action — which made it even more invitational and made it much less of a mind-blocker. Yet, he was not flippant about it either. As a Christian, he did what he did with confidence and joy, but he did not make light of it. He saw it as a very serious action, done in a very dramatic way. He knew that he had attempted to destroy some real idols of society.

Dan told me about the Catonsville action. I was amazed to learn that almost three hundred people had been invited to participate in the action of the Catonsville group and only nine said yes to it. There were married people, single people, priests, religious, nuns.

One nun made the mistake of asking her mother superior if she could participate. Imagine! How sad that a nun still felt that she had

113

to ask her superior if it was all right for her to follow her conscience! How totally bankrupt religious life is if it totally destroys one's freedom! How contradictory to the Gospels!

I also got to see Tom Louis, an artist, an incredible guy, who was part of the blood pouring with Phil in Baltimore and the Catonsville action. He inspired me tremendously and a real friendship began. Tom, by the way, received a six year sentence.

Then I got to see Phil Berrigan. He was in the county jail and there was this big piece of glass separating us which made communication difficult. But I told Phil I was getting ready to organize something and he got very excited about it. I'm not sure he understood the whole thing I was saying, but there was some communication and it was a great visit.

I went down to Virginia and visited a Madonna House about sixty miles south of Washington, D.C. It was a kind of retreat house, one set up by the famous Baroness Katherine de Hueck. I was trying desperately to get my head together.

Netty was holding the fort back in Milwaukee. I called her several times, but I'm sure she was worried to death about me.

I finally returned to my job which, surprisingly, was still waiting for me. I had taken a somewhat legitimate vacation or leave, so at least I was in no jam there. I don't think I was looking for excuses to quit the job, but I began to see how out of place I was in working with the blacks. Not that I couldn't relate to them, but it became increasingly important for them to recognize that they could be doing the same job I was doing.

My mind was almost totally on the action. What action? How? I was impossible to live with. My mind had no room for anything else.

Finally I decided I would do it all myself — some time in July, maybe, I would simply enter the draft center and destroy all the records I could get my hands on.

I told Netty.

That ended that. She was pregnant again and she made it unmistakably clear. If I did anything as crazy as that, she would leave — period.

Well, I figured if I got other people involved, perhaps she would not be so adamant. The first person I contacted was Father Jim Harney, a newly ordained priest from Boston. Then George Mische, one of the Catonsville 9, contacted me. It amazed me how the word was getting around.

My first plan was to go into an induction center and to destroy the blood that was taken from the possible draftees for blood tests. I thought it completely vulgar that doctors, the medical profession, whose responsibility it is to preserve and defend life, should spill blood in order to prepare men for murder. I wanted to destroy the blood that was taken from my brothers to find out who were the best, the most physically fit men to be chosen to murder and be murdered.

I had no doubt about my right to do this — to show the doctors that this blood is on their hands, that the blood of the innocent is on their hands.

So, I began casing the place, finding out how to get in, and when it was the most busy, etc. Father Jim Harney came out because he was interested. Jim was offering Mass at Casa Maria and we did a lot of praying about what we should do.

Finally, we decided to wait for a while and to contact more people. Jim went back to Boston to talk to people there. He arrived one day with three more Boston priests. We talked and talked and then we decided we would have a retreat on the East coast. Father Paul Mayer, a Benedictine monk, returned from Panama, managed to get us a Benedictine camp for a weekend up in New Jersey.

I'm sure that most of the monks at the near-by monastery didn't know what was happening. The camp was just finishing its summer activity. It was vacant when we got there and all the facilities were open to us. It was truly a beautiful spot.

About sixty people arrived from some twenty cities. Wild! The word simply got around, and yet, no one had any fears about being exposed. These were committed people who simply trusted each other. These were people who by their very presence proved they were willing to place their lives in jeopardy — for the sake of their consciences. We were there, essentially, to plan another action. But we also meant to seek effective ways of resistance in all the communities represented.

Netty and Brigid were with me. Brigid was just two weeks old. She was beautiful and I was grateful I had waited for her.

The retreat was an incredible experience, just beautiful. There was a great sense of joy and community, of working together. We alternated as cooks and with the other chores. We sang lots of songs and did lots of swimming and lots of just plain relaxing.

It was a group of Christians who were really taking the Gospels seriously and who really had a sense of life. Nearly all were Roman Catholics — married people (there were a few other children present, though no other family agreed to participate in the action as such), single people, priests, nuns, brothers.

Dan Berrigan spoke the first day. He spoke about community, but dealt primarily with the prophet Jeremiah. The whole idea of Jeremiah made it imperative to speak the truth, to confront evil. Regarding the community that is the Church, the first Christians were witness to her, saying no to Caesar. The obligation of the Christian to say no to

Caesar has not lessened. Murder, injustice, are being perpetuated by Caesar, committed in Caesar's name.

Dan challenged us to consider what the new mark, the new sign of the new People of God will be. What will be the sign of the Church? What makes the Church important?

His answer, of course, was that the Church needed to be the sign of life to the world. Love had to be central to the Church, the mark of the community of faith. When the Church loses sight of that mark of love, she is no longer really the Church. A Christian is recognized by his love. Christians are known by the way they love each other.

Law must never be at the center of the Church. The Church must never make claims on the lives of men. The Church must never be a Church of claims, but rather, she must be a Church of invitation.

And so, Dan and the rest of us discussed how the Church was to be reborn, how we, as Christians, could exemplify the beginning of new birth.

George Mische did a lot of political analysis and no one could doubt his ability and qualifications. George is a brother of Gerry Mische who developed Aid for International Development (AID), which was very concerned with Latin America. George himself had worked in Latin America for four to five years.

I say these things to show what many people, many Americans, may not know — that the men of the Catonsville 9 and of the other actions are not empty-headed fanatics. These were and are men and women with a broad educational background and a wealth of experience, people who have visions, but not people of unrealistic idealism. Nor are they people of hopeless pessimism who destroy out of despair and thrust their gloominess on the rest of mankind.

The radical community at the Benedictine camp also asked me to speak. My subject was voluntary poverty and the need for people to adopt a whole life-style of poverty, of really living it. I spoke of the need to develop hospitality houses, not just for the sake of hospitality, but as a tremendous experiment, as an external sign of where our minds and spirits were going.

It seems so evident in Scripture, in sections like the Acts of the Apostles, that the early Christian community obviously sold everything and shared everything.

Community houses are also the best way to develop resistance, of getting people into the movement. A lot of young people don't know what to do, but one thing they cannot miss is that people must feed the hungry. There is nothing unreal about that. Feeding the hungry flushes out the rhetoric and flushes out all the political hardware that seems to be floating around in so many groups, especially Church groups.

Feeding the hungry puts you into the raw gut of the thing and puts you right into the middle of it and takes out all the abstractions and makes it very concrete and real. And so I encouraged people in the group to open hospitality houses of their own.

However, at the end of the talk, I announced that I was going to initiate a public action to protest the war. I told them I was inviting them to participate, that I wondered how many in the community there would be willing to act soon. I had told Netty about my plans and by this time she was not only ready to accept what I felt I had to do, but she herself said that she was willing to participate. But, of course, someone had to be with the children.

Then, during our meeting, came the news of the police brutality at the Democratic national convention in Chicago. The police in Chicago gave us one more push. Dan Berrigan had said that if the system showed signs of change, we had to be open to seeing them. But Chicago certainly gave us no indications of a change.

I announced to everyone that a meeting would be held the next morning in the old barn down the hill for those who wanted to participate in an action. Anyone who would walk into that door would walk in because he wanted to act.

A few of the people in the barn the next day were there not because they wanted to act but because they had already acted. Father Dan Berrigan, George Mische, and Brother Dave Darst, all of whom had acted at Catonsville, came to the meeting to share their experiences and to help us plan our action.

Eighteen people said they were ready. The questions that remained were what, how, when, and where. We all knew the why. The Gospel was compelling us to speak, to condemn death and destruction and to stand up for life.

Almost from the beginning, our planning centered in on the destruction of draft files. Probably because many of us were on or in the Milwaukee scene, we decided Milwaukee was the place. We knew that one accessible building in downtown Milwaukee housed nine draft boards.

But another reason why we chose Milwaukee was that we decided the Midwest had to have an action. All the radical activity not only originates in the East — usually the East is the only stage for it. True the West coast is also alive and aware. But the staid Midwest ordinarily has little to say or rather, rarely takes a radical stance on things. The Chicago police riots also helped us decide on the Midwest. Daley had to be dealt with in some way, shape or form.

Yet, we felt we could not hit Chicago. At that time we considered the city impossible, too uptight, too difficult to break. The draft boards there would be too difficult to study. We had to act soon — and no

117

one would ever suspect radical action in Milwaukee. True, Father Groppi had somewhat changed the "gemütlichkeit" image of the city, but for the same reasons that Milwaukee was so racist, it was also hawkish — passively and apathetically so, but hawkish just the same.

Although only fourteen of the eighteen acted in Milwaukee, the other four eventually acted in one way or another or at least got deeply involved in the resistance movement. Of course, that number has grown many times over and that is the revolution that is taking place. That's what the establishment, the power structure, the system cannot understand. We are a non-violent revolution and we are determined to win and we are going to win and we are winning. Many draft centers have been invaded and the reports have not even been made public. We still need imagination, new ways of confronting the system, the system of death and destruction, but we will find the ways.

Two young women wanted desperately to partake in our action. Both of them were immigrants, and the one had only two weeks left in the country before her visa was to run out. We simply had to refuse the other girl's request. We all agreed — except for herself — that the jail experience would be too difficult for her to bear alone. We knew the political implications, we knew well that the system would come down hard on us, with a vengeance and a hate that would demand a great deal of support among ourselves to survive at all.

One priest was with us up to three days before the action. The reason I mention him is to indicate that he was perfectly free, as all of us were, right up to the action. Our action was truly invitational and everyone had plenty of time to say no. I believe that if any action is co-ercive and not invitational, the action is not non-violent, nor is it creative, nor is it going to be for the ultimate good of society.

Many people came forward from various parts of the country to participate in one action or another who were emotionally geared up to act. However, some of them were not able, or didn't appear able, to deal with the consequences. I was part of many meetings in many places and constantly advised people not to act unless they had their heads together.

A lot of people in this country have not faced just how many actions have occurred, just how broad the resistance movement is. With more and more conspirators, we'll fill the jails and the system will not know how to work. I don't say these things lightly, but we have to laugh about them, too. We are talking about dancing and laughing and singing. We are talking about appearing mad to human beings in the face of much more insanity, which is much more death. If we lose our sense of humor about these actions, we lose everything. A sense of humor is missing in the movement in many places and we get saddened and down. With that attitude, in our condition, in our times, we'll all go crazy.

But can you imagine a couple of hundred of us on trial for conspiracy? The system couldn't handle it. Then it would truly be a whole community — a community of risk. Then it would not be a personal risk, but a community risk. But we must be creative. We haven't even begun to become creative.

We must turn this system into something human. We must stop the madness. The system must change. We must resist and most of us who are resisting have chosen the war as the prime target. The people who say that we would be revolutionaries even if Vietnam were allowed to be free are right. They are right because our imperialistic, colonialistic display of power and ghastly military might is only a symptom of the sickness of our way of life. The war is merely an example of the bankruptcy of our system. But the war is at the top of the ladder. It exemplifies our sickness.

By protesting the war, we of the Milwaukee 14 and of the other actions are protesting much more. We are saying that our priorities must be reversed. We cannot tolerate a system which considers roads more important than homes, a system which says that wars are more important than roads, homes or people, a system which has people at the bottom of the ladder.

But why don't we work within the system? First of all, in a way we are, because there is no other way! We are, because there is no way we can really work *outside* the system. Secondly, the war is now — not tomorrow or next year, but now. Even if we could get fifty people elected, and not all the money in the world could do that, it would take time, years of time, and then, the system has a way of swallowing up even those who begin with the best intentions and highest ideals. Perhaps we have to begin a new political party. Of course, we have to continue with the basic work of the Gospels, feeding the hungry and housing the homeless. But we cannot remain at the basic and primitive level of Christianity or we are not people of our times.

But we of the Milwaukee 14 were saying that we could not wait. We were saying, "We cannot accept this war right now, we will not support this war in any way or in any form." We had to be resisters, we wanted to show our absolute and total and outright resistance. We were saying no, and we were becoming hunted persons, letting the F.B.I. have a dossier on us, not being afraid, not being up-tight about it.

Being a hunted person is not a myth or a romantic game. Being a hunted person means that the system knows who you are and where you are all the time. It means being suspected all the time and blamed immediately for any disturbance. It means putting oneself in the bag of being a convict, an ex-convict, and once an ex-con, always an ex-con. It means being pulled out and questioned everytime a burglary or arson or bombing takes place. When I was in Kansas City for a talk after our action I was yanked out of my bed in the middle of the night because a bomb threat had been reported somewhere in the city.

These are the implications and repercussions of freely letting the system come down on you. These are the rewards of the person who engages himself in the work of bringing the system down. This is why people must have their heads together before they act.

Prison itself would be bad enough and we knew we would eventually end up there. Yet, we were not copping out. We were convinced that we were winning by going to prison. We felt that if just one person were won over by our going to prison, we would still be winning. But we knew that amid the outrage and shock, many would be moved by the men who were willing to put their lives on the line for what they believed. And many there have been.

Nor did we have a glorified, romantic view of prison. We knew it would be hell, and I knew it would be hell for Netty and the kids. But I, personally, was deeply and fully convinced that prison was the right place for me to be. Note, I said me. I never said "for everybody."

Obviously, many in the movement do not agree with me. Black brothers and sisters, many of them dear, close friends, have retreated to the old methods of violence. Hell, we've got enough of that in history. Pick up a gun and you end up with an arsenal. I don't care who you are. I don't care how outraged a person is by the violence and injustice around him.

I think we have to become Davids to bring down Goliath. David was a smart cookie. I don't agree with his use of violence, but I admire his imagination and creativity. I'm saying that we have to become so smart in our use of non-violence that we can trip this big guy up, we can pull him down.

Not that I'm against all systems. A system will always exist, but a better system must be originated. Human nature cannot be changed. Man's tendency to selfishness, what we of the faith have labeled as original sin, is very much a part of us. But the Gospels invite us to a style of life and this style will always be systematized to some degree or other.

Usually that means the majority rules, the common good must be served. But some things can't be done for the common good. You don't kill someone for the common good. You don't put someone in the electric chair and say it's for the common good. That's where the Church, the Christian is important. I can see the Christian community, a small minority, standing up to the whole country. It's better to have one person stand up to injustice than no one at all. If the Gospels teach us anything, they

120

teach us fearlessness. Non-violence makes us fearless, and non-violence is at the heart of the Gospels.

We of the Milwaukee 14 were not without fear. But as someone said, to live in fear and not to be afraid is the final test of maturity. When we got back to Milwaukee, the real work began. We had the people, qualified people, and perhaps this is a good place to identify the 14. The identifications fit the men at the time of the action.

Father Robert Cunnane, 36, studied for the priesthood in the Congregation of the Stigmatine Fathers. He studied philosophy and theology in Rome and was ordained in 1959. He was an assistant in a parish for several years and for five years served the Espousal Retreat House in Waltham, Massachusetts. He was co-director of the Packard Manse Ecumenical Center in Stoughton and Roxbury, Massachusetts. Bob was active in the peace movement for at least four years and had collected draft cards at a burn-in in Boston's Arlington Street church the previous October. He was among those who testified at the Spock trial.

Father James Harney, 28, was an assistant at St. Jerome church in North Weymouth. He worked with the poor of Baltimore as a community organizer. He co-founded the Baltimore Inter-faith Peace Mission. On October 16, 1967, he turned in his draft card at the Arlington Street church resistance service in Boston. At the Spock trial, Jim testified on behalf of Michael Gerber.

Father Anthony Mullaney, 39, a Benedictine monk of St. Anselm's, Manchester, New Hampshire, has a doctorate in psychology and has taught at St. Anselm's and Boston University. For the year previous to the action, Father Mullaney was stationed at Warwick House in Roxbury, Massachusetts, an inner-city house, church-operated by a team ministry.

James H. Forest, 26, was the co-chairman of the Catholic Peace Fellowship. In 1961, after two years of active duty in the United States Navy, Jim was discharged as a conscientious objector. He served at St. Joseph's House of Hospitality on the Bowery in New York and was managing editor of the "Catholic Worker" for a short time. Jim was administrative secretary of the Committee for Non-violent Action, and of course, has done a lot of writing, especially for the Catholic press — "Critic," "Ave Maria," "Sign," "The National Catholic Reporter," etc. Jim was married at the time of the action, his son was five, and he and his family lived in East Harlem, New York.

Jerry Gardner, 24, had graduated from Marquette University in 1966 with a degree in mathematics. Jerry was teaching and working for his master's in Milwaukee.

Bob Graf, 24, a native of Milwaukee lived and work in the Casa Maria community. He had studied to be a Jesuit for some seven years and received a degree in philosophy from St. Louis University in 1967. He was continuing his studies in sociology at Marquette.

Fred J. Ojile, 23, was a draft counselor and church program organizer for the Twin Cities Draft Information Center. After graduating from Catholic University as a seminarian, he attended Law School at the University of Minnesota. After a year, Fred left the university and became a full-time organizer in the resistance movement.

Brother Basil O'Leary, 48, a member of the Christian Brothers, the religious order of teaching brothers, was the real scholar among the 14. He has a M.A. from the University of Chicago, and a M.A. from Loyola, and a Ph.D. from the University of Notre Dame. At the time of the action, Brother Basil was the chairman of the economics department and associate professor of theology at St. Mary's College in Winona, Minnesota, with articles published in a number of periodicals.

Father Larry Rosebaugh, 33, a member of the religious community, the Oblates of Mary Immaculate, was working with us at Casa. He had served as a pastor in St. Paul, a religion teacher in Duluth, and an inner-city priest in Chicago.

Don Cotton, 24, studied with the Glenmary Fathers for five years, but left after serving one year among the poor of Appalachia in their native habitat, and one year of serving emigrant Appalachians in Chicago. He received a degree in psychology from St. Louis University and was pursuing graduate work there in urban affairs. He was also the co-chairman of Students for a Democratic Society at St. Louis University.

Reverend Jon Higginbotham, Jr., 27, was a minister of the Founding Church of Scientology and the Church of American Science.

Father Alfred L. Janicke, 33, a priest of the archdiocese of St. Paul-Minneapolis, was very much involved with the poor, especially alcoholics.

Doug Marvy, a Navy veteran with a bachelor's degree in economics, was pursuing graduate degrees in economics and mathematics.

It is important to point out most specifically that there were no psychological misfits among the 14. None of us had ever been in trouble before. We were not addicts, or "hippies," or communists, or alcoholics, or any of "those kinds of people." We were "straights," squares, men trained and schooled and working within the system.

But these were the 14 — the 14 who caused an outrage in the minds of middle Americans in middle America, the 14, or I should say, the 13, who touched my life more deeply than I can possibly say.

When we got back to Milwaukee we went to work. We began to case the Brumder Building at 135 West Wells Street in downtown Milwaukee. We needed other people to help and we found them. Some of the people who helped the most were not among the 14.

We needed a person from inside, a person who really knew the draft boards. We had sketches, charts, and even excellent photographs taken by a tiny camera. When we went into that building, we knew what we were after and where it was. Every person had his job to do.

(Those of us from Milwaukee were responsible for the casing. In essence, of course, we were planning a robbery, sure, except we didn't want the loot. We didn't want anything for ourselves, we didn't want to make any profit. It wasn't like robbing a bank!

All we were trying to do was get into that building without hurting or harming any person in any way. That was the deepest concern of all of us.

And I have to put this footnote in here. I feel sad if any harm did come to any person. I feel bad about one woman in particular, one of the women responsible for cleaning. Obviously, these women were and are good women, not anywhere near being responsible for the war. We had to be non-violent, and it would have been better had the whole action been aborted than that any harm come to any of those persons. Otherwise we would have betrayed everything we had to say or anything we were trying to do. It was good that nothing major happened, but I am sad that anything happened, that the one woman was a little fearful for a time.

But a big part of the action was the casing of the place. We spent almost three weeks, day and night, watching the building. We watched to see who came in and out of the Brumder, taking notes, watching especially for the time that the fewest possible people occupied the building. It was our conclusion, after three weeks, that the time the building was the most vulnerable, when the fewest people would be around, was early on a Tuesday evening, from 5:40 to 6:30.

A major reason for the Tuesday choice was that the near-by jewelry store was closed Tuesday evenings. We weren't interested in jewels, you see. We were interested in draft files because draft files to us were the symbols of the death of millions of people, particularly of the young men who were murdered as a result of files like these.

The draft for me and for others in the 14 was the mustering of men for death. And I don't think, though many may think differently, that in the future, mankind can ever give that power again to any government, the power over life and death. That power belongs to no-one except to the Creator of life. The draft law represents false power in the hands of Caesar, as is the power of the state to sterilize men and women (twenty-six states in the United States claim that power). The right to inflict capital punishment is illegitimate power in the hands of Caesar. The same is true of the power of the state to determine whether or not a mother can have an abortion. These are questions which touch deeply the souls and the minds and the spirits and the bodies of men and women — questions which can be answered ultimately only by a person and his Creator.

We cannot give power to Caesar illegitimately. I believe Caesar has some right to exist and has a right to being. We as a people give power into the hands of a few to make our lives more human and to make sure that the common good is taken care of. That's why we have judges and juries and the law and Congress and the Senate and a President and all that. But our lives can be truly jeopardized when we allow power to be misused in our land.

In fact, that's where we find ourselves in our time. I consider the draft law, particularly the draft law, knowing what this war is about, a false power of the state, destroying the minds and taking the lives of the young of this society. I think history will bear me out, that the death of forty-six thousand Americans and the hundreds of thousands of Americans who have been maimed, mentally maimed, scarred from this war, are going to have a mark on the history of the country. I have found young men, twenty-two years of age, coming back from Nam, as they would say, who are now on the Skid Rows and in the jails of this country, young men who cannot live with themselves and who may never be able to live with themselves because of the incredible experience of war.

I say this because of our first-hand experience with the poor. We found so often that when someone gets broken or feels that he's failed, that he cannot continue to live the certain pattern of life prevailing in a society like ours and hence, he often ends up on what we know as Skid Row. I speak particularly of the young today. It's a frightening thing to know there's another generation of young men about to appear on Skid Row, particularly when you see they are victims of a war, victims who perhaps had no part in nor even made or were able to make a free conscious decision to get into the war. I know a young black man who was coming to the meals at night. Part of his abdomen had been destroyed by gun fire. But more than that was destroyed. You only have to look into his eyes and you know the anxiety that has happened there. I couldn't begin to tell you the number of stories similar to the tragedy of this young man.

Then there are a number of young men who act as if their lives had stopped. They go around without any direction for the future. Often they become alcoholics or heroin addicts. When we see something in contemporary history like what we have heard in the last three or four months at My Lai, then the horror and reality of the war comes home to us. Then we as Americans in all sincerity exclaim, "We wouldn't do that!" Well, we have Hiroshima and Nagasaki behind us, too, names which shake us, but we don't dare face them and acknowledge them for what they are.

So today we find ourselves deeply shaken, and we have to live lives that do not face reality. So it's no wonder that young people are despairing. I have been across thirty-five states and I have talked mostly on campuses. I find the young despairing, looking for a future and it's no wonder that we have what we call a counter-culture being developed in the society, or what some would call the hippie community. Young people have dropped out of the society and have taken on the drug scene as a way of surviving. This is a very frightening reality facing all of us. Then I look at the young people in our neighborhood alone, the hundred or more youngsters within a four or five block area, children between the ages of nine and fifteen, who have no place for recreating. We must begin to see the resources we need to rebuild our city, to make possible a future for young people who do not have a future.

The war goes on. It continues to demand that men be inducted into the service against their will. The choices the draft leaves open to young men are so few, though many think there are a lot of choices. If a young man at eighteen years of age is not able to articulate his conscience, if he's not able to articulate his faith, Baptist, Catholic, whatever his faith would be, and he's not able to get a conscientious objection status, he has little chance. And often he doesn't even know that the phrase "conscientious objection" exists, that he has those rights. This is most often true of poor people. Often they feel their only choice is to go to war, regardless of how they feel personally.

Many young men feel they are faced with only one choice, that of leaving the land of their birth. How strange that Europeans who came to our free shores to get away from the draft or from intolerant systems, now have sons who are leaving the United States for the same reasons.

These facts must be dealt with. If we face reality squarely, we cannot be surprised over our sons and daughters who joined the Weathermen.

We are building a revolutionary army in this country because of our foreign policy. Our young people have their eyes open and they see only violence, a government of violence, run by the military. The visible sign is war — war is proof of what we are.

Then, suddenly the Federal Government sets up a commission, a group of men and women to study violence in the United States. And all of a sudden we are told that America is violent and crime is going up. But, on the other hand, we murder on a global scale, we have built the war machine, we have troops in over a hundred countries. The Pentagon controls at least eighty per cent of our tax dollar. That's not sane. What priority does education have? Or welfare? What per cent of the tax dollar? That's got to be insane for any society. So our economy is

125

built on war, and we have no way of thinking how we can change it. And I don't have to be a great statistician to understand that. I just have to look at what the domestic policy is, and have to look at our priorities from the Senate and Congress of this country and begin to see where we are going.

Now we have our eyes opened to pollution. We are moving into ecology. Our lakes are being poisoned. Our resources are being sapped up and we are taking resources from the other parts of the world. Some experts are telling us that by 1973, we will have real famine in mass proportions in some parts of the world. We as a nation are six per cent of the world's people. But we have great resources. We live off of about sixty per cent of the world's income — or at least control that much. That has to change. How do you change it? I don't know.

The only thing I can say as I stand before you in this late, late time as a person, as one man, that I felt I would betray the very fact of my own humanity if I had remained silent. I could not let my children face what we are facing today. If I wished to speak and to live and to be a sign of gentleness and hope as best I can be, I had to speak. I am not a saint. That's foolish. I am a bone of your bone, I am flesh of your flesh, I have the same problems, anxieties, I don't have any clear-cut answers at all for anybody. I feel simply that certain things are demanded to be human, and I see the action of the 14 as an act of self-defense to my very humanity. God help us, we had nothing else to do, or nothing else we could do — I don't mean to do, but I mean could do. Other ways of protesting had been stolen or else they had been co-opted by this society.

The rights of the First Amendment, the right of free speech, is an incredible right, as I began reading recently in *Point of Rebellion* by Judge William Douglas of the Supreme Court of the United States. Judge Douglas is not some extraordinary mad man in this society. He's a judge, a man much like Jefferson, a man of the people in his own time, and Lincoln and Thoreau, and Eugene Dobbs. That was America. That is America. That's the kind of madness we are as a people, that we have the possibility, that we are free enough in this society to allow one another free speech because we trust we will act on behalf of the common good.

All right. Now, what I did was breaking the law, yes, I was conscious of it, yes, I was conscious of it. It was an act of destruction. It was burning paper. It was burglary. I was interfering with the Selective Service as stated in this court. But on a state level we call it burglary. Theft. All right. Paper. Theft. All right. It's theft. Arson. I have a hard problem with that, I don't understand it, except I did burn paper. Helped burn it. Poured the gasoline which was made from the formula in the Green Beret Handbook of how to make home-made napalm. That

126

is sane in our society, that is legitimate. We actually allow, you know, the writing of a prescription like we give a sick man medicine. We say here you are, young man, here's a prescription on how to make napalm so you can destroy people more quickly.

That's insane. I have got to tell you, that is insane, and that's why I am here today. I must tell the jury, too. These are hard times. And yet, you know, yes, I broke the law, and you are stuck in a sense. Or we are all stuck. Maybe I am stuck with the law and probably am, and maybe you are not. However, I once studied in history that the jury had a great leeway in this country, that they could make the law. What I did was wrong. Nevertheless, the weight of making the law may be on your shoulders. That weight may be in your hands, as to how you understand what law is, and what order is.

I'm not sure I understand what law is and order is, except it's working on behalf of the common good, I know that, and saying the right things when they must be said, and, hopefully that's at all times. But these are tough questions, and all this comes to bear with the fact of how we were planning to do these acts which so outraged people. But we had to do them. Because for so many years, we had watched — we had watched the death of our brothers in color, live, on our TV sets, in our own dining rooms and would go on and eat dinner after it. We had been dehumanized and didn't know it.

We continue to poison our own society today. Many societies are facing the same problems but I speak to where we are, and I speak to where we are because I think we have the possibility of being that society which I think can render a real hope to mankind and womankind. The great thing about America in my mind is that never has a society had such dimension and pluralism in it as this one. I say we are a rich land and a rare land. I don't know any society with our quality of people and maybe that is why we are where we are in this century, because someone else might have ended up in our situation anyhow.

But we are black, we are white, we are yellow, we are red, we are Catholic and we are Protestant and Jew and gentile of any faith, Buddhist. We are Chinese, we are Russians, and we are Americans — American Indians, American first-born. We came as slaves, we came as men and women running away from tyranny and happy that we could find a home, and we came at many times. I came late. My mother was here before me. My grandfather was here. He went back. Some of your fathers maybe went back or relatives went back. For whatever reason.

But the beautiful part of this country is that we can build a society worthy of man, worthy of woman, worthy of the name human, made in the image and likeness of creation, Creator, and I think these — this to me is the heart of why we are here. . . .

But let me go briefly into a little more detail on the planning of the action, the casing of the building. Anyone has the right to enter his draft board and ask to see his file. If a person can draw, and if he has a good memory, he can sketch the exact position of the files, the 1-A files.

The week-end before the action we had another retreat, all fourteen of us. We met on a farm near Milwaukee and went over detail by detail the job each of us had to perform. We had a problem figuring out how to get inside the building what we knew was required to get the files outside of the building.

About all we needed were burlap bags. We had screwdrivers, too, but we didn't need them. I don't think they were used at all.)

Of course, we sang a lot at the retreat, and we broke bread together. Liturgy was always a part of us. The liturgy was always so marvelous, so powerful, so rich. And the reading of the Scripture and the strengthening of our lives and the bringing of our lives together. The liturgy was always a source of strength because it showed that we were one with one another. Twelve of us were Roman Catholic, including five priests and a Christian Brother. Reverend Jon Higginbotham was a Protestant minister who told us he had not broken bread since he had observed the racism in the South, but here he felt he had found a community of faith and he felt one with us. Doug Marvy, who also joined us in our liturgies, was sort of an adopted Christian, though his background was Jewish.

But we did more than pray and sing. It was at this retreat that we prepared the statement of the Milwaukee 14, printed in the beginning of this book. Jim Forest had done a lot of work on it since our retreat out East. But all of us brought our ideas to it. The statement represented the various fields we were working in, some of us working directly with the poor, others pursuing scholarly interests, others "religious" in the Church sense, etc.

But the statement fits into the history of resistance in this country. It is a very American statement, in the same tradition as the Boston Tea Party or the Underground Railroad. It spoke clearly of civil disobedience, very radical, very much in keeping with American history.

(Other details had to be planned. The biggest problem of all was how to confront our cleaning friend. She was our great responsibility, to remain human to her, so we went in — or planned to send in the most gentle of men in the community, Father Larry Rosebaugh, and Brother Basil O'Leary, who had been a teacher for some thirty years in the area of theology and economics, but a gentle man, that they could talk to her. It would be natural to introduce themselves, but what should they say to her? And so we practiced these things.

Some of us went up during the week before the action to find out what kind of woman she would be, how she would react with our being there at a time when people weren't supposed to be there because the offices are locked. She was a very gentle woman — very gruff, but very gentle and we were able to talk to her.

But we weren't prepared for another person to come down into that building, and that was our biggest problem. How do you confront a person in those circumstances? We always felt that if there was any danger to anybody, we would abort the action. If there was going to be violence with the police, if police would come up not knowing who was in the place, thinking it might be a robbery of the jewelry store, we would stand on the top of the stairs and have our hands up and be prepared to be taken into custody. We weren't going to run away. We were prepared to give our lives up. The main thing was to gesture, to point out what we were about.)

On the day of the action we all met at one location on the south side of Milwaukee. We all dressed up because we wanted to have our dress be signs of who we were — not kids getting into trouble, but persons willing to bring everything we were in the community. And so the priests wore Roman collars, I wore a suit and tie, etc.

And so at this apartment we worked out the final details. Let it be known that our final preparation for this act was a liturgy — we celebrated a Eucharist together and went forth two by two as Christ sent his disciples.

Each pair took a different route to the Brumder building. We had over a half hour to put in. I walked with Jon Higginbotham and I was so paranoid that I thought every person on the street was a cop or an agent. It was just foolish paranoia but I'll never forget it. I kept thinking what a strange looking person John was — an older man with long hair and a beard and a pot belly and a Roman collar on. I was sure everyone was looking at him and suspecting us, and, of course, a lot of people knew me and I was really scared someone would come up to me and start rapping about something or trail along with me. You know, I could see it all, here I was at the most dramatic moment of my life, within minutes of getting inside the building, and . . .

What a walk that was! John and I walked through poor white sections of the city and then visited Milwaukee's War Memorial building on Lake Michigan. The visit was like a pilgrimage to a shrine. It was a prayer that somehow our action would help keep another war from happening.

The only thing I had in my pocket was a toothbrush — everyone of us had toothbrushes — and I had the Scripture and my rosary beads. I felt that was all I needed to keep me alive and human and I'll tell you, I used those beads in those days more often than I probably had since I had come to America. I've used them a lot since, too, and the Scriptures.

Then came the incredible part — arriving near the Milwaukee Journal building, seeing my friends appearing at different corners. It was downright funny.

We had planned to get all the 1-A files, plus the duplicates. Although the act was primarily symbolic, I really mean it when I say I would have done anything to stop all induction from that center. Even if it meant ripping up every piece of paper in that place, I would have done it and faced the consequences. The message had to be brought home.

We had practiced making the napalm from the formula in the Green Beret handbook. We knew the burlap bags would burn well. We must have had some thirty to forty gallons in big red cans in the truck. We figure we dragged out some eighteen bags containing some 10,000 files. When we lit the pile the flames must have leapt some fifty to sixty feet. We regretted not having a stoker to stir up the fire.

But we were burning up more than files. We were burning what's so real in our society — not files but fear. We were saying "we are not afraid." Young men allow the government to keep a file on them out of fear. And so they go out and become murderers out of fear — against their own consciences.

Doug Marvy, dressed as the janitor, was the first one in the building. He had no trouble distributing the bags to the proper doors. Jerry Gardner was second and it was he who had to give the OK sign. Brother Basil and Father Mullaney were to confront the cleaning lady for the keys. We were prepared to take down the doors, but the lady was either convinced or overwhelmed. She gave them the keys without any physical violence after they told her we were there to save American lives.

Each pair of us had an office to get — to ransack in every sense of the word. We knew that technically if a file is disrupted it should be redone, a process of over three months. Obviously, draftboards cheat, they are very dishonest, and this particular draft board continued to induct almost immediately.

We didn't have enough men to go around for all nine draftboards. But we didn't have to pry anything open and the keys opened all the doors we wanted to get into. After that the job was easy. The 1-A's had red tags on them — symbolizing death? — and our friends had sketched the position of the cabinets for us.

John was terribly cool, smoking a cigaret, and we filled up sack after sack. We figured we had about twenty minutes in there and we knew we could do a creaming job on the place.

A great liberating feeling overcame me once I was in the building.

I knew I was breaking the law, directly confronting it, really making a free choice.

But then the unexpected happened. The woman who supervised the whole cleaning operation paid us a visit and began shouting and screaming. We treated her as kindly and non-violently as possible, but she did have to be held and for that we are truly sorry.

Her visit stopped our party, just as we said would happen if the unforeseen happened. Everyone began moving out with his loot. The first things we did after we got to jail was to send the two ladies flowers and a box of chocolates. However, the policemen came and picked up the chocolates as evidence. Perhaps they thought we were going to poison the two witnesses of the act.

Then another incredible thing happened. After we got down to the lobby a well-dressed black woman came in. She saw everything — our equipment, the bags of files, files spilled up and down the stairs and on the floor of the lobby. She looked at us, smiled, and went upstairs, and never appeared as a witness. That woman really understood! That woman was hip! She saw everything and could have identified every one of us.

Then we broke outside. It was quiet out there. One of my friends told me that just a few minutes before a squad car and a patrolman had passed. Doug Marvy was the man to get us across the street by stopping the traffic, with his body if necessary.

But we had no trouble getting across the street to a little green triangle with a flower pattern in it. We came across the street shouting and singing and making all kinds of noise. Again, it was liberating and we truly felt a great joy, as anyone who saw the videotape can attest. We felt spurred with new life — as if we were running home.

As soon as we got out the building, the truck with the napalm arrived. The truck had been parked illegally a half-block away and it was ticketed. Later it was hauled away by the cops and we had a devil of a time getting the truck back.

After we piled up the files, we made sure there was no one sitting on benches across the way. Often old men sat on those benches and we wanted no one to get hurt. We had decided that if there was any chance for someone to get burned we would not have used the napalm.

Across the street was the campaign headquarters for Senator Gaylord Nelson and a lot of people were looking out wondering what the hell was happening. We poured the napalm and lit the files and the flames danced high. And above it all, the American flag flew strong and proud.

I knew the police were going to come and anything could happen. We could be gunned down or the police could come and beat the hell out of us. But I didn't care. I didn't care! I prayed aloud a prayer of thanksgiving and led the singing. We linked arms with one another and read some Scripture — and waited — waited to be arrested. That's how free we were.

And the false gods, the false idols of society burned. We could have walked away. I'm convinced we could have gotten away with it. But we felt it was necessary to stand and say no, totally, to say who we were.

We must have stood there about fifteen minutes. Then a policeman on a motorcycle pulled up and made a call from a phone on the sidewalk. He called in that a bunch of hippies were having a bonfire on the triangle.

The fire engines came and about four paddy wagons came to load us up. I was still making a statement and one of the policemen said I was under arrest by my own comment. Then he said we were all under arrest and the police began to handcuff us to get us into the wagon.

The police took one look at Doug Marvy, the man dressed as the maintenance man, and told him to get lost. But Doug insisted that he, too, should be arrested. Fantastic!

The police were kind yet at this point because they truly did not understand what was happening. It was September 24, election time, and although it's illegal, I noticed many of the cops wearing Wallace buttons.

(The whole action took place in full view of the media — TV, radio, a movie camera, newspaper reporters — which we had alerted to be there. We felt it was not just our act, but an act which belonged to the public. It was an act for the public — to judge in terms of their own lives. That's where the values were and had to be met. Unfortunately, our press contact was prosecuted for conspiracy, even though he was not as involved as the law people said he was.

It's very interesting, although we didn't realize this until after the action, where this took place. It took place at the Brumder Building, which I heard some time later, used to be called the Joan of Arc Building. Somehow this is an interesting echo of history.

Also, the place of the burning! We were burning the files in a triangle dedicated to our war dead. What a way to celebrate these men's lives! To say, in a sense, we will never kill again. To say that this war has been the most senseless in all of history. Not just in American history, but in all of history, where men and women have been ill-equipped to come up with new solutions.

Now, of course, you confront the Second World War and you see a different thing. What would have happened in Hitler's time? Who would have stopped Hitler? The trouble is that good men are quiet when they should not be silent. The biggest tragedy in history in my mind is that good men made good excuses for doing bad things. Unlike the early Christians, the Christians of Germany were silent at the birth and the building of Hitler's regime. Perhaps if the German Catholics or Christians would have responded with their lives as we are responding today, we would never have had a Dachau and all the names that have come from that. The point is that in this time in America, there's still a chance for me to come into a court like this and be respected and to respect the judge. That's the beauty of it all.

I know many feel that sometimes the law finds itself on the side of war-making. But I think we can do more than reform the law. I think the law can be a real service to the community. All we need do is think of the difference between how we conducted this trial and how other trials have been conducted. I realize I must respect people's lives wherever they are, and the punishment that will come on me is not an easy thing because I can cry just like you and I get scared just like any one of you.

But I know that we do what we are doing because I know we have to. It's not that someone had a gun to our heads or coerced us into it, but we had no other way of acting and remaining human.

We had tried other ways. In February of 1968, after I was conscious about the war, after I had fasted against the war at St. John's Cathedral in 1967, I started a forty day fast outside this Federal Building to confront our community on the street. The fast wasn't an absolute fast like the one of the year before, but it was a fast of forty days on one meal a day which was in essence much like the poor of the world live on. I was trying to be one with the poor and trying to understand their life, their plight. Many, like the men of the street and the women who come to the meals, often live right here in Milwaukee on only one meal a day. I began to understand why, and how they felt. But most of the time I stood alone each day in front of the building. I was out with the public who didn't understand, who were angry and called me a communist. Some would knock me down on the way back to their office, if they could, or spit or throw paper. But some would come and say that they understood. There were all kinds of sides, and some were amazed, wondering what I was doing there. But it was a great experience. One could really understand the inadequacies of all of us, because we all have them. We all have our failures and faults and inadequacies, and that was coming across.

But other ways of protesting were not speaking loudly enough. And now we found ourselves in a serious business. I will never forget the pulling of the bags of files across the street. It was almost like pulling a fainted person. Have you ever pulled anybody who fainted? You know, the whole weight is there and the body is like a rock. Somebody said a bag weighed eight hundred pounds. That really surprised me. But it felt like you were saving lives, like the bags were dead or half-dead victims. I remember Bob Graf saying when he was taking the files out that he felt he was saving a drowning man.

I remember something Father Mullaney, the Benedictine monk, said when he was in the State Court. When someone asked him why he did what he did, he said, "Because St. Benedict did." Benedict lived in the sixth century and Benedict knew he had to do what he was doing. These times demanded us to do acts that were rather extraordinary and have a certain amount of punishment to them and would not be easy for the community at large to accept. But they were important because they go beyond our own time. They go into the future. Why we were chosen we don't know. I couldn't tell you why I am here, except that I know there is a journey and an echo that is now making sense. My life in Ireland could have been just as real as the lives of my brothers there now. But I am here.

So we burned the files, and we sang and we read the Scriptures. We read from St. Luke about the burning of the earth and about dividing family against family. We were saying that our families would not always understand and there would be great division among us and wars, but that hopefully we could keep these wars from being bloody wars. Perhaps there will always be wars of words and disagreements on a political and ideological level, and not wars of the fist and the gun and so on.

And so that day we stood before the community, waited for arrest, readily admitted that we had done what we had done, and were brought into custody. But the weight of the community came down on us quite heavily, as all of you know. Over $400,000 of bail on our heads, and it took us nearly a month to get out of jail.

But it was a good month. I am glad, because I could never have understood what jail was if I had not been there. I might have been free had my name been important or had I been rich. People would have come to my defense. But as Jim and Gilda Shellow and anybody else who was associated with them at that time know, these were hard times in my life. My wife and kids were outside. The community that I loved, the people that I loved, the work that I loved, were now apart from me, and there was a wall between us, and bars. It was very tough and I went through great pain and anxiety. But it was a growing month.)

It was an education. From the moment we got on to the paddy wagons, even before the great sense of joy and accomplishment had disappeared, we began eating the raw reality of the belly of death — the police, the rawness of the society we were saying no to.

We were still pretty high. We knew the whole city knew and we could almost feel the foundations of the city shaking. We could feel inside what the action was doing to people, what was happening, that something fantastic had just been let loose in the city.

And the word went to other cities, twenty of them. The message was, "A beautiful sunset over Milwaukee and the wieners are frying."

The paddy wagons brought us under the Safety Building in Milwaukee, into the jail. We were all thrown into the bullcage, a big pen, an open thing with bars all around and no chairs or benches inside. Other men were tossed in with us. The total inhumanity of the prison system was very real, immediately.

After a couple of hours we were placed in another bullpen. There were a couple of chairs and a bare bench and cold, terribly gray-looking walls. The whole prison scene, dull as anything, was there to break you, with no sense of humanity, not built for humans, not for even a dog. Maybe a mad dog. The whole inhumanity of how men and women could work in that, how secretaries could go home and get married and have babies. They must be stones to confront life at that level, to face a constant death scene.

We waited in this second cage for a judge to come and set bail. They started taking us out one by one and filling our forms and taking our photographs. They put a number around our neck and took our picture and got our fingerprints. That's all part of being a criminal.

At ten or eleven that night, Judge Christ Seraphim appeared, a man to my mind who exemplifies the power of the devil, a man who is surely possessed, less than human, who daily sends men and women to houses of correction which are inhuman.

Seraphim is just one more example of that breed of men who can push buttons which napalm and burn people and not have a whimper about it. He is part of the system that's able to do what it did at Nagasaki and Hiroshima and what we are doing in Vietnam. We must talk about what makes men like that, men like Johnson and McNamara and Nixon and Laird, who can justify murder because we might be attacked as a nation, because of freedom, because of economics.

Not that there aren't good judges and good senators and good lawyers and good teachers and good journalists — sensitive human beings — good men, like bishops, but who have no courage.

When Judge Seraphim came before us he had vengeance written all over him. He was very honored to come before us, as if we were the peak of his career.

I thought I would try to meet this man with some kind of humanity. I was very quiet, perhaps because already I was sad, very sad, about where we were and that what we were seeing was actually true. What we knew was wrong before, we were now experiencing.

135

Anyway, I ended up with some $32,000 bond on my head — a bond that defeats the very purpose of bond and convicts a man to jail before a trial. And then Seraphim said the most vulgar words I've ever heard. He said to me, "Say hello to Netty for me," and he laughed with a vicious, diabolical laugh.

Seraphim made me realize that evil can possess anyone of us — if we allow it in the beginning. We start by compromising, then we begin to fear losing our positions, and then the desire for more things, materialism, grows stronger, and then we become trapped.

That's why Dan Berrigan said he had to say no to this war right from the beginning or he might have gotten to a time when he could never say no. We must all begin to say no to evil and to false power.

Imagine the power, for example, of one man to come in and totally, arbitrarily set a ridiculously high bail on our heads. Democracy. American justice.

Well, we knew that we could never raise over $400,000 worth of bail, that we would be in jail for a long time, that we'd have to begin contesting the high bail. That meant getting a lawyer immediately. I had seen a lawyer a couple of days previously and scared the man half to death. He was tied into politics — his father was a United States Congressman. That is the problem, good men make excuses for doing bad things.

After the ordeal with Seraphim we were led to another bullpen and then finally to individual cells, a little coffin about six feet long and about four feet wide, with a wooden bench, a commode with no cover, and a roll of heavy brown paper which was supposed to be toilet paper. Oh yes, a water fountain hung on the wall right above the commode.

We couldn't see any of the other prisoners, just steel on all sides. These were hard nights because you had to sleep on that bench. The bareness of the cell described the state of my mind and soul. We were truly men naked before society. We had laid ourselves bare, and all I could think of was my wife and my children and my future with them.

The first night, all I could do was to pray the rosary. I knelt down on the cell floor and I began the rosary, aloud! I'm sure it was the first time those guards and those damned walls heard the rosary, but we prayed it all night. Jim Forest said he hadn't prayed the rosary for four years previously and one of the priests said the same, but I had the equipment for the night. It kept us human, it kept us sane, it kept us relating. We sang some songs, too, some psalms and other hymns praising the Lord. The guards said nothing. They didn't understand us. We were just too much for their heads. As days went by though, they seemed to relate to us and become just a bit more human.

The first thing they did the next morning was to make us parade, three by three, on to this brightly lit stage. There must have been some two hundred and fifty people in there to see the show, policemen, special squads, plainclothesmen, F.B.I. guys, and whoever else was around.

When they called your name, you were supposed to step forward and turn around for them. But they made a mockery of us, calling us fascists, communists, shouting from the crowd. When someone was identified as a priest, shouts came back, "He's no priest!" Incredible! Vulgar! Inhuman! The curses they hurled at us!

The "line-up" as this is called was no fun. But we had to keep up a sense of humor. That was most important. I remember hearing Jerry Gardner say as we walked out, "Well, I guess I'll never make it with the defense department." As long as we could keep laughing, we knew we could make it. That's what it was all about anyway — a damn joke, the whole thing. If you think about it, it's really a joke that a society like ours, as sophisticated as ours, is so bankrupt that it handles its problems in this way, that this was the only thing they knew how to do, the only way they knew how to beat us. These pitiful, pathetic men, hired by society to inflict a form of death to humanity, death to man, death to conscience and to life itself.

The next day they brought us out of the individual cells and into the court and we saw the community for the first time. Netty came and Brigid, my baby daughter, and what a scene of embracing! Father Jim Groppi was there and a lot of other people. One of the policemen, upon seeing all the beautiful girls who came, asked how he could get in on an action like ours! The visitors brought some newspapers and it really blew our minds reading the stories and the reactions.

But we were not flippant about our action. We had already begun fasting which we continued for ten days. We wanted the whole experience to be spiritual, to have spiritual meaning and power.

The lawyer whom I had contacted and scared before the action, the United States Congressman's son, was the only lawyer there representing us to get our bail lowered. He, of course, did not know the action was going to happen, but one of the sergeants chewed him out and promised to prosecute him and have him kept from the bar. He was just freshly a lawyer, a pretty good guy, a little radical in his own head, but they had him shaking.

Perhaps a hundred young people, all wearing red M-14 armbands, were in the courtroom when we walked in. I tell you, our faces were filled with tears. We felt that something had been born and that we were a part of that birth. We knew we had real friends out there.

The young people did nothing but sit quietly, smiling and beaming their support, but when Judge Seraphim came in, he blew his stack and threatened to clear the courtroom if there were any demonstrations, verbal or non-verbal. The whole scene was really funny. None of us had anything more to say. It was just beautiful.

Later we tried to get Judge Seraphim dismissed from the case. He said he was very honored to be dismissed from the case, and that he had set bail that high in order to keep the streets clear of anarchists.

The high bail, of course, was an act of vengeance, a punishment. Bail is to make sure a man turns up for trial. A man is innocent until proven guilty and only then is "punishment" inflicted.

Really, at some point in this country, men like this should be taken out of office and retired somewhere on some common farm where they have no power. I wouldn't have them killed or sent to Siberia, but just to some common farm to graze, to dig in the earth for a living, to learn about life and humanity, to give them a chance for salvation. By leaving them in office we are denying them a chance for salvation.

After the court scene they again put all fourteen of us in a common cell and this was a great thing. We really rejoiced. It was the first time we had seen a bed in two or three days. There were several beds, with mattresses, plus some army cots. There was one toilet and three sinks. We lived like this for at least two weeks.

We fasted from solid food and some drank only water. We wanted to extend ourselves to the suffering world, to those who were fasting involuntarily.

They had taken all our personal things by this time. They watched us while we took a common shower but they let us wear our own clothes. At first they denied us any papers, but then they allowed us to have them. We were permitted to see our families twice a week for one hour. This was the hardest part for me — seeing Netty and wondering. I wrote her letters every day, some of which and parts of which, appear in the next chapter.

But things got personal now. I ceased being political. I was more into myself and I was tossing myself back and forth as to whether I had done the right thing. The only thing that kept me sane was that I had to do it, the system made me do it. My enthusiasm was dampened but my mind was sure of one thing — I had to do it. I was convinced that even though I had a family, a wife and three children, even though I was deeply wounded and dying inside because of fear for them, I knew I did what I had to do and this kept me sane.

In those two weeks together we were really hard on one another. We were doing a lot of dialoging. We made strict demands on ourselves. We'd run seminars, sitting on the floor. We got deeper into one another's lives. After all, there was nothing to hide. We spent a night on each person, digging into who we were and where we were going.

We had other seminars, too. We kept a kind of university going and for all of us it was a scholarly experience. Brother Basil, for example, was a reservoir of knowledge, especially on the subject of technology and where it is taking us. We had only a few books to deal with, so most of what we discussed came out of our heads.

Somehow I got a hold of some poems and pictures and I had a tremendous yearning for the mountains and the woods. The things I used to take for granted I began to appreciate much more, like the little light through the bars. The bare, bare cell really got to me.

But the people on the outside helped tremendously. One night Father Groppi and Dick Gregory led a group of more than a thousand people past our cell. Right in the middle of the night. It was fantastic hearing these people shout, even though we didn't know at the time who was leading them. It was so beautiful. We climbed up on the bars and tried looking out, though this was forbidden.

It seemed as if every night a group of young people assembled across the street, sometimes as many as a hundred of them. They came with lighted candles and stayed in silence in the cold evening for a three-hour vigil. These are the people who kept us alive.

Across the street from the Safety Building a peace sign arrived on a window in an apartment building. Every night a candle was lit there, across the street in the free world, where people lived whom we didn't even know. I used to think about what it might be like to live in a divided city like Berlin. Being in jail was like that, looking out to see people of hope, people showing us hope just by a symbol.

The people outside considered themselves free, but I couldn't help thinking that they were not free either. We were both in jail, we were both in systems, and as long as men are in jail unjustly in a society, no one in that society is really free.

One day, in the middle of the afternoon, my wife and son Willie were out there. They shouted to us (which they weren't supposed to do) and again we climbed on the windows. They started dancing on the sidewalk for us and they were beautiful! Willie was really something!

These were hard times and beautiful times. New and deep friendships were beginning to happen because of the action. A Jesuit scholastic took leave from his studies to establish a defense committee. An office was established, with a staff of volunteers, just to work on our behalf.

We were all quite overwhelmed by these people, by their generosity — people who didn't even know us but who were deeply concerned. We received letters from all over the country, beautiful letters.

And, of course, dear friends like Fathers Dan and Phil Berrigan sent us letters of hope and joy. It was a great time for life because we were so close to death and a great time for hope because we were so close

139

to despair. These were precious times, times in which I grew the most because I had to open myself, to get very deeply into myself. I couldn't fake it. I couldn't fake the future which demanded total honesty.

Our display of joy and enthusiasm, the visitors on the street, the shouting and laughing back and forth did not put us in favor with all the guards. One time, one evening, it appeared as if our air supply was cut off. The air got thick and actually appeared yellowish. Even the little place in our door that we looked through was sealed off. We did worry and we did get panicky because we believed we were using up all the oxygen. It was like a bad scene from "The Battle of Algiers." The one thing we thought of doing was to turn on all the water faucets, hoping to get oxygen that way. This went on for almost three hours, a truly nerve wracking experience. Somehow we got word to the warden and the air improved.

I think it was about this time that one of the 14 got a letter out to a priest out East who got a message out to Ted Kennedy. I guess the letter went to other people, too, like Cardinal Cushing. Perhaps it was coincidental, but we seemed to get better treatment after that.

It was over two weeks before we were finally allowed to exercise in the bird cage, a huge cage on top of the Safety Building. It was great to walk around and see the city, but the caged-in feeling was awful.

Then suddenly we got our own place, a whole tier, with various cells. We used one as a kind of dining room and we even had a TV which was given us by the attorney I finally chose, James Shellow. Apparently the officials told Jim that he could give us the TV but he would never get it back.

But we kept up our reading and seminars, even though after a while other prisoners were thrown in with us.

Soon it became obvious that we would not be there much longer. After a month, my bail came down to $10,000, still by far the highest of the 14.

Chapter Eight

City Jail
September 25, 1968

My dearest Annette, Willie, Brennan and Brigid,

I love you — I love you. Everything here is fine, except perhaps very humiliating. Process in court — dehumanizing. Everything went off fine, thank God!! I miss all of you very much. Pray that you have faith and courage to keep on!! That will help my pain a great deal. Let's leave all of this in God's hands from now on. I love you — I love you.

Mike XXXX

Milwaukee County Jail
September 26, 1968

My dearest Annette, Willie, Brennan, and Brigid,

I love you all — I love you all — I love you all very much. How are you all doing? I pray that these things have quieted down somewhat for you. Oh, Annette I love you. You have such great courage. How are you doing, Willie? I miss you a lot and Brennan and Brigid too. As for me, things are better now. We are settled here in jail. They put us in what they call the County jail annex — one large room with fourteen beds — three sinks, one drinking fountain and one toilet. The sheriff came to see us today. Sheriff Purtell. He is a Catholic — he is rather nice. He gave us a radio and gave us a table and four chairs. We are on a fast and that is shaking everyone up. Really we are feeling quite good. Thank God.

141

I guess the mail is really coming in. You can come to see me. I asked today. Anyone from the immediate family. So check it out by calling. See when you can come.

We are meeting with some lawyers this afternoon. We will work out strategy then. Try and get people to fill the courtroom tomorrow afternoon at 1 p.m. We saw the march last night. We tried to make noise so you could see us. Our cell is on the third floor on the corner of *ninth* and *state*.

Annette, as it looks from here, we should be out by Sunday, unless there is a problem with bail. We are hoping we will be able to have Mass here today or tomorrow. Mass or no Mass, you are in my thoughts and prayers always, and always my spirit is with you. Give my love to Mary Joe, Sam, Juan, Chuck, Bill, Kathy and all our great friends.

Annette, maybe you should write my Mom, but if you think it better to wait for a while, do so. She probably will get very worried. Maybe better not put her through that yet. How about Dorothy Day and Karl Meyer, Ammon Hennesy? They should get our press statement.

I'll stop here, sending all my love to you and the boys, and Brigid Mary. I pray that we soon will be united as a family again.

Peace and Love,
Mike XXXX

For immediate release
Statement to the court, September 27, 1968

With regard to the present hearing:

1) We have serious unresolved questions regarding the morality of so vast a sum of money being used for us when so many are dying by violence, starvation and lacking adequate shelter, clothing and medical care. In solidarity with those who fast involuntarily, and in order to better seek the guidance of the Holy Spirit, we have confined ourselves to a liquid diet since our imprisonment last Tuesday. We are continuing our fast. Our situation reminds us of the chasm which separates poor from rich: prison is for the poor.

2) Our imprisonment has a providential dimension. We have found it an enriching experience, permitting us to enter more deeply into the measuring of freedom, love, joy and hope. We understand better than ever the transcendence of self and comfort which true freedom requires.

3) We have not yet obtained legal counsel. Though we have been advised by several attorneys, we need to discuss our legal situation with

other lawyers before making commitments which will unalterably affect our case. We expect to have retained counsel in the next several days, provided that we have access to the telephones and have adequate time for group meetings with prospective counsel.

Therefore, we ask a postponement of these proceedings.

The 14

To Annette, with Love always and for the Press.

Mike XXXX

Annette, I want to see Jim Shellow. Mike

Milwaukee County Jail
September 30, 1968

My dearest Annette, Willie, Brennan and Brigid,

My deepest love to you. It sure was a joy to see you tonight after court. My spirit was low at that time as I am sure yours was too, but somehow tonight — 10 p.m.? — things look a little different. It must be God's grace. He sometimes lets us feel rock bottom and then He assures us that He has not abandoned us, but is only trying us as to how deep our faith in Him is. When I came back to my *cell* or our *room,* I became very depressed and then began to cry. Larry started to read the Psalms to me — not knowing I was crying because I was hiding my face. The Word seemed to hit me like lightning bolts and my faith began to return. Then the community asked me to speak about a hospitality house and its importance, the works of mercy and their importance, and you know I found myself speaking like I never had before. Everything I have tried to do up to now seemed to have great meaning. Little pebbles in God's *Holy Plan* always open to His friendship and guidance. These past six days have been strange ones. Days which have changed my life — a time to think through under tremendous pressure and stress — a time to pray, though very hard — a time to think about you and our family. My love for you Annette could *never be described.* What courage you are being given in these terrible times of distress. We must continue to beg God our Father never to abandon us. If we always do His Will, He has promised us that He never will. My love to all at the house, Annette, and a special love to the boys and Brigid. Let us pray that God, our Father will soon bring us all together again!!

Love, Love, Love, Love,

Mike XXXX

143

My dearest Annette, Willie, Brennan and Brigid,

My deepest love to all of you. I pray and hope you are all fine!! Annette, I must say you really looked beautiful today. I am sorry we could not have a visit. It was also good to see Mary Ellen, Diane and Dave present. It up-lifted my spirits. The bail hearings were what I expected, though I had some hope for Judge Ceci. However, I am sure it is in God's Holy Will that things be this way. Annette, the more God seems to try me the more my faith increases. It is all so very strange. I hope you are not getting too discouraged at this point. I am sure it is very hard. I pray that God our Father will soon deliver us. I love you, Annette. I love you. May God continue to fill our lives with faith-hope-love-peace, joy and courage.

How are things at the House, Annette? Did you write Pat H.? I think that is a good idea that he come and take care of the house. He is a good man. Have you had any contact with your Mom or Dad? I pray that they are "O.K."!! I would never want to harm them in any way. They are good people. It was good to see Mike Z. on the stand yesterday. Tell him I am most thankful. Annette, in case I forget, would you or someone bring Larry's breviary or my short breviary? Would much prefer Larry's. I hope we have a visit Friday. It is so beautiful to see you. You are my spirit. You know, Annette, I have been reading a lot of Sacred Scripture these days and you know it is almost like I am reading it for the first time in my life. Reading it at the house has meant so much, but here in jail it means so much more. I never realized that so many of the prophets and disciples were in jail. I really don't know where that puts us, but I guess we are among the *crack-pots for Christ*. Ha!! Even in jail we have a sense of humor. I close here Annette, until to-morrow. "I love you with all my being and spirit."

Peace, Love and Joy to you and the boys
and Brigid,

Mike XXXX

* I know that we will soon be united!!   Mike X

My dearest Annette, Willie, Brennan and Brigid,

My deepest love to all of you once again!

I am writing this letter late in the afternoon. We are not allowed our watches, but I figure it is about 5 p.m. The rest of the fellows are

144

in court this afternoon, all except me and Father Bob Cunnane. So, things are rather quiet around here and I am sure they will be for a while. They took us up on the roof this morning to get some fresh air.

How is everyone around the house? My sincerest love to all — Mary Joe, Juan, Sam, Kathy and Chuck. I miss them all very much. It was quite something seeing all those young people walk by last night. Oh, by the way Annette, thanks for the sweater. I love you, I love you, I love you.

Annette, at this time, it is about 10 p.m., October 2, 1968. We had a long talk tonight on our personal life. Sure are great and beautiful men here, as I am sure you are aware. It was truly beautiful to see the vigil tonight. Those young people no doubt are the hope of America. Despite these hard days America one day will be a great and wonderful land. We did a lot of reading together tonight. Also, Sacred Scripture, Gandhi and Nikos Kazantzakis. I suppose you know all about the bail thing. Just goes to show us how bad things are here in this country right now. We must continue to work and pray. It is just a matter of time and I am sure the bail will be reduced.

You know about Friday — my bail hearing? I pray things will be better then.

I hope things are good with you. We must remember the poor and suffering of the world at this time. We leave things in God our Father's hands. Annette, did I tell you about our beautiful Mass last Sunday morning here in the jail? A Cap. OFM, Father Gerald Schmidt from St. Benedict the Moor, said the Mass, the priests here were not allowed to say Mass. Anyway, the Mass was beautiful!! I am thankful for my rosary these days. I get in about 15 decades each day, asking God and His Mother to take care of you and bring peace to men. Annette, most of the letters you keep at home open and read and *if possible,* answer, or have Mary Joe answer. You just send me a letter, "OK"!! I close here, Annette, sending you my spirit, with every bit of love I can muster. I love you. I love you. I love you, my darling, my life.

Mike XXXX

Milwaukee County Jail
October 3, 1968 10 p.m.

Annette my love and babies!!

It sure was a joy and a great hope for the spirit seeing you out on the sidewalk in the vigil tonight. You raised my spirit and brought many tears to my eyes. I said a rosary while waiting the vigil. God love all those wonderful young people.

No doubt I look forward to tomorrow with great anticipation! Perhaps it will be God's Holy Will that bail will be reduced. I will pray continuously throughout the night. I read all of St. John's Gospel today. I found some great insights. I will share them with you when I get home. Tomorrow is a great feast for those who live or try to live voluntary poverty, the *Feast of St. Francis*. I pray that he hears our prayers. He has been a special patron of mine for many years. I am sure he will answer my prayers tomorrow on his feast day.

Annette, I stopped writing for a while and started reading the Holy Scriptures. The book of Revelation by St. John. Here is what I am reading: "I know your tribulation and your poverty and the slander of those who say that they are Jews and are not, but are a synagogue of satan. Do not fear what you are about to suffer. Behold, the devil is about to throw some of you into prison, that you may be tested, and for ten days you will have tribulations. Be faithful unto death, and I will give you the crown of life." — Tomorrow is the *tenth* day.

With these words, Annette, I am going to call it a day. Good night, my love and God's Holy Peace be upon you and the children and all those at Casa Maria and the many good friends of all of us. I love you and will until time ceases and beyond.

I love you, I love you, I love you. I really have so few words to express myself, Annette. I love you with my spirit, soul and body, every fiber.

Peace, Love and Joy,
Mike XXXX

Milwaukee County Jail
October 4, 1968, 10 pm
Feast of St. Francis

My dearest Annette, Willie, Brennan and Brigid,

Annette, seeing you today, this morning in court, our visit this afternoon and at the vigil tonight, renewed my spirit once again. You are truly beautiful, a torch, a light in this time of darkness. What courage and hope you give to me. We had a beautiful liturgy here tonight ending our day, and celebrating St. Francis' feast. A great calm has come to all of us. God surely is allowing us to go through great experiences. His spirit is constantly being revealed like I have never known before — in all my religious experiences. Annette, I would like to get the Breviary when you have a chance to drop it off. Also, perhaps a history of the

Roman Catholic Church. Oh, I must tell you about the good Mr. Shellow. He brought us a *TV* and we are allowed to keep it *here* in the jail. God, we are so grateful. Make sure Jim is thanked outside. OK? He is such a good man. You were all remembered in our prayers tonight, other prisoners and guards, also. Chris Jones' book looks OK — read some of it today. Thanks so much for it. Glad the paper came out today!! Tell Fr. Fredrick to come and see me. I put his name on my list. He has been so good to me in the past. He is a good religious man!!

My love again reaches out to all of you — all you fine people, may God bring peace and love to Milwaukee through all of you. May new life be reborn in America once again. Without violence. May men live as brothers and sisters regardless of race, color or religion and may we move on to a new future where all things are possible.

I love you. I love you. I love you. May God, our Father watch over our boys and Brigid and help them grow to be men of peace, love and joy.

Good night, my love, may your sleep be always restful!! God our Father will always keep watch over you and Mary His Mother will be patroness of our home.

Love, Love, Love always and ever,

Mike XXXX

Milwaukee County Jail-H-Annex
October 5, 1968

My dearest Annette, Willie, Brennan and Brigid,

I hope everything is fine with you. Today for me has been rather a quiet day. I had a haircut — not bad. We all did quite a bit of reading today. I read some of Chris Jones' book. You know it really is good! Also read some of *A Penny A Copy,* some great stuff in it. I read the article in the paper, two papers today. I was rather pleased and surprised. I got a lovely note from Warren and Mary. God love them. Is Warren out of the hospital? He did not say. He included Ignatius O'Connor's quote: "Christ has promised to those who get involved that they will be unbelievably happy, never overcome by fear and always in trouble." How true!!

How are things with you Annette? Did the kids get home? Any word from your home? Write when you can. I'll write you each day. I have been reading about farming a little bit. I will have an opinion later, have to let it sink in. We will have Mass tomorrow. I look forward to it eagerly. Will remember you and all our good friends.

Good night, Annette, my love to you and our beautiful family. Love, Love, Love, Love — Always!!

Peace, Love and Joy,

Mike XXXX

Milwaukee County Jail-H-Annex
October 6, 1968

Netty My Love!!

Greetings to you, Willie, Brennan and Brigid. My deepest love to each of you. Today, Sunday, has been a very quiet day, boring, to say the least. Mass this morning was good. You know who said Mass? A brother of Father Gracen, OFM Cap., from St. Lawrence seminary. He is now pastor at St. Benedict the Moor on 10th and State St.

Mr. Shellow came in to see me this afternoon. Sure was good to see him. Said my case goes before the Supreme Court in Madison tomorrow, 10:30. I'll be praying all day!!

How are things at the house, Annette? How about the boys? Brigid? I miss you all so much. My heart sometimes feels like it will drop out. But, I guess this is the way God wants it for now. Hopefully, it will make up for the immense suffering of our world right now, like the thousands of children who are lost everyday because of war and starvation. He has promised us a hundred-fold if we suffer voluntarily. There are many things I do want to write about to you but for the moment they must wait. I have got to think them through yet. And pray over them. My love to all at home and all our friends. Love, Peace, Love, Joy, Love, Peace, Peace, Peace.

Mike XXXX

Milwaukee County Jail-H-Annex
October 7, 1968   11:30 p.m.??
Feast of the Blessed Virgin
Mary of the Most Holy Rosary

My dearest Netty, Willie, Brennan and Brigid,

I love you, Netty. I love you. I love you Willie, Brennan, and Brigid. Today has been a strange day. One of despair, hope and now peace. Hope because I thought good word would come from Madison, but I guess you read in the paper that nothing will happen until Thursday. We shall continue to pray and trust!! Annette, many things are going through my mind,

148

so, I am going to attempt to write them down for you. OK — (love you, I love you!!)

What I will write here in this letter is just for you my love and the children. I am writing it tonight because I plan on giving it to you tomorrow. Oh, Netty, I look forward to your visit with great anticipation!!

Tonight we saw a documentary on India and her famine on Channel 10. It really frightened me. Why I am telling you this is it has something to bear on how I feel about my being in jail.

You know Annette, ever since our action, I have been going over everything I have ever done in my life. Asking myself *Why* the hell am I in jail. In other words, what the hell am I doing here. May sound crazy, but that is the truth!! I got to the point of even regretting the action, perhaps because of the despair of jail. But the longer I am in here I am beginning to see a little more clearly and understand everything a little bit better. Seeing that film tonight on India brought things more into focus. On the stand last Friday, I told the court that I love America and I meant it. And I will tell the court and jury when the time comes that I not only love America, but I feel sorry and sad for America because we have allocated 71 billion dollars for defense next year. While people in the world starve to death, children are blown to bits and a world continues to live in fear, etc. I don't conspire against America and I never would! I have risked much to say these things, perhaps a good future!! But I love America and I want my children to be proud of this land. There is so much more on this question I want to say but I just don't have the words yet. Please God, we will have an opportunity soon both of us to spend some time to talk more and see a little clearer what I mean!!

There is a question of the church and priesthood which I am thinking about and thoughts I want to share with you. I'll deal with that question tomorrow. I love you. I love you. I love you. My spirit reaches out to everyone at home. My love to all. Kiss Willie, Brennan and Brigid for me. I love you Annette more than the world could ever imagine or understand!!!!!

Peace,
Mike XXXX

Milwaukee County Jail-H-Annex
October 8, 1968
7:30 p.m.   Tuesday
My dearest Annette, Willie, Brennan and Brigid,

I just got through reading the letters. I could not read them for a while. My spirit was too low — many tears, etc., but now thank God, my spirit has lifted a little. Your visit today was a gift. Oh, Netty, you good

149

and beautiful woman, God love you — I just don't have the words. I love you, I love you more than the world could ever hold. I love you, my love!!

My mother's letter was rather interesting. So was your mother's. She — your mother — is a beautiful woman. God love her. I thank you deeply for the Breviary. I will make good use of it. Many prayers are needed for all of us and our world!!

I was going to talk to you tonight about the Church and some of my thoughts about the Church but I really don't feel up to it tonight. I'll try to write something on that tomorrow.

Annette, I was thinking about the family which came recently. You know I really think it is too much at this time. You must call all the agencies and churches and tell them not to send any more people at this time. Feeding some people each day is OK.

I must go to sleep now. We are told to go to bed — lock up, they call it!!

Peace — Love — Joy. I love you all!!
You are my flowers!!

Peace,

Mike XXXX

Milwaukee County Jail
4th Floor   H-Annex
October 9, 1968

Netty my Love — Willie, Brennan and Brigid,

Your letter today was beautiful. It not only raised my spirits but gave me new life. I love you, Netty, more than anything, any person in the world!! I love you — I love you. I love you. Tonight we watched *Dr. Strangelove* on TV. What a frightening movie!! It was almost too real!

Today was a day of prayer — said the entire Office. We had vespers and compline in common. Sung it — beautiful! The priests are not allowed to say Mass!! But we do have Mass on Sunday — a priest comes in! I believe I told you that.

Well, Netty, tomorrow is an important day. I believe we will have good news. We'll start prayer early in the morning — 6 a.m. We'll continue throughout the day!! I am writing this in the dark — since the lights go out at 10 p.m. Now there is a dim light in the hall so I can just about see. I love you. I love you. I love you. Larry was happy to hear all the news. He has been so good for me. A beautiful human being. Also Bob Graf. I'll close here, though I could go on saying I love you until there is no more paper left. And you know I would still find some place to write I love you.

Mike XXXX

150

Milwaukee County Jail
October 9, 1968 10:30 p.m.?

A poem for Netty my *Love*

For so long I thought I saw flowers with many beautiful petals but now the sun has risen and I realize that I really only saw a beautiful plowed field. Now I feel spring in my bones and nourished by two weeks in jail, beautiful green flower buds are appearing on the ground. They are more beautiful than I could have ever imagined. They hold a beautiful summer for us both. I love you, Netty.

Mike

My love Netty   Mike your husband!!

Milwaukee County Jail-H-Annex 4th Floor
October 10, 1968, 10:10 a.m.
St. Francis Borgia

You Netty, Willie, Brennan and Brigid are my sunshine!!

Thursday it is — quickly moving towards the appointed time for my hearing at the Wisconsin Supreme Court. I was up before dawn saying Matins and as dawn broke, I had already said Lauds and a rosary. Oh, Netty, there is a freshness in the air. Almost like spring. It looks like a beautiful blue sky and bright sun. I have great hope for this day — good news is in the air — all the psalms are joyful, "Sing to the Lord a new song, for He has done wondrous deeds." Read Psalm 97 taken from Lauds today.

Netty, I tried to write you a poem last night — not very good — but I am going to keep on writing. I love you and I want to find ways of showing and expressing my love for you. I promise not to make them mushy. But, I can assure you, they will come from my heart, sometimes from my gut!! My love for you has awakened anew, like spring flowers, more beautiful than I have ever known. These past years have been filled with so much. We really never had enough time to nourish our love or perhaps "express" it is a better word. This will never happen again. I love you. I love you, more than dreams could be filled. What beautiful children we have been blessed with. Peace, my love, let us go and pray for unity for us both — Soon — soon — soon — Peace.

Mike XXXX

Milwaukee County Jail-H-Annex 4th Floor
October 10, 1968, 11 p.m.

My loves — darlings, my hope!! and dreams!!

To hear your voice tonight calmed all my fears, brought a new peace once again. Though I was sad on hearing the news (my hopes were very high today). Your voice and our *few words were new life.* Oh, Netty, my love, these are trying times for us both, but my love for you takes on new meaning and a new direction. I love you with every fiber of my body and spirit. It is amazing how we hold together here. We turn to one another for hope and peace and joy. What great men these are. Such as the likes have never been born before!! I term all of this a new cosmos of life. It is being born and you, Netty, and all those wonderful people who are working on our defense committee are a part of this cosmos, plus the young people who stand each night in the cold, vigiling for us. Our love to them. Tell them that they give all of us great hope!! New thoughts today. The reason for *war,* for military fear in our world (over-kill, etc.) is that we never have had an army of peaceful men-*resisters,* of non-violence-men who refuse to carry guns, of men who refuse to go to war, of men who face prison rather than make war. I believe this is about to happen if it is not already happening. A new kind of men is being born men who have and will sacrifice much for peace. If the intellectuals begin to do this, the country could never stand for it. All the *brains* in jail! Brains are $$ in this country. Am I dreaming? Are there such men in this land? Nevertheless, they must come forward, otherwise we will end up a military state and perhaps a nation-world of *fear,* or a parched earth. "Evil prevails when *good* men do nothing," so much education to be done. This jail experience is perhaps a form. The ridiculous bails, etc., or are people at the point where they don't give a damn? It seems in Germany people were so afraid that there was so very few who would stand against Hitler's machine. They would surely lose their lives! And as a result 6,000,000 Jews died!! Am I crazy or is what I am saying the truth? I believe I am right. It seems to me it can get to a point in a nation (because it did in Germany) that a government has so much power the people become as it were paralized in *fear* and so are not able to resist *evil!* Perhaps they even know it is *evil.* Racism in this country, in the South, is a very good example where white folks who perhaps did not agree with racism, said nothing because if they did, great bodily harm would come to their lives. The questions of military power, police state, private property are similar things. A sick fear is in our land and good men must face it straight on. I am as fearful as anyone else. I have too much at stake. You, Netty, whom I deeply love and the children who are my very life!! This venture, though a hard one, *must* be made!! My prayer is that men and nations will rise and say NO to WAR, to MILITARY STATES, by raising an army of NON-VIOLENT men, men who are not afraid to die, or to face high bails, or prison. This to me is man's only hope. A hope which gives us no choice at this point, if man is to have a future on this planet. My hope, Netty, is that we have not waited too long and that perhaps we are in time. Men are not too dead yet. There is a spark of life some-where. Perhaps among the young. This army I am talking about can still be possible. An army of NON-VIOLENT men who will refuse to carry guns, but instead face the courts, prisons and high bails. Armies of violent men have given us history as we now experience it. We have no other choice other than the one we have embarked on.

Netty, I hope you can read this scribble. The thought just came out. It must have been your beautiful voice, you know. You just inspired me!! I love you, I love you, I love you. I tenderly touch you with my spirit. This is for you Netty. I will give it to you tomorrow when you come. My love, my love, my love, courage, faith — words — they just don't say it for me. Shalom, Netty, sleep with my spirit. I am with you every moment I possibly can!!

Love, love, love always

Mike XXXX

(You are my four flowers whose colors are like the rainbow.)

!!Love!!

Milwaukee County Jail-H-Annex
October 11, 1968   9:45 p.m.
The Divine Motherhood of Mary, Mother of God

OUR FATHER

My dearest Netty, Willie, Brennan and Brigid,

Today Netty you looked like the sun and as beautiful as the moon on a magnificent summer's evening in Wisconsin's north woods. Oh, my love, you were like an apparition, and Brigid, oh Brigid, my beautiful daughter!! Your words and your touch were so warm and kind. On reading this evening's paper my soul was oh, so sad and sorry for some of those people who wrote against my person. I feel my soul is being dragged through a sewer!! I feel sometimes my heart is being sliced in pieces. I just can't describe the sadness sometimes, but thank God for prayer. After night prayers tonight my spirit has been lifted and a new peace has come over me. The Psalm for compline tonight was 85. "In-cline your ear, O Lord; answer me, for I am afflicted and poor. Keep my life, for I am devoted to you; save your servant who trusts in you." . . . "Grant me a proof of your favor that my enemies may see, to their confusion, that you, O Lord, have helped and comforted." It is so strange Netty, during the day my spirit is very restless, but at night a great calm comes — peace is a better word — over me. The peace can't be described. That is why I know I must have no fear regardless of what they do to me. I love you. I love you. I love you more than the world

153

or the hearts of men could know or dream of!! You are the cause of so much of my joy.

Jim Forest showed me a diagram of what love is today. I will draw it for you. He describes it as each person being an island: Mike — Netty — Willie — Brennan — Brigid, with water between the islands. Most people think the only way to communicate is to travel by boat from one island to the other. But suppose someone burns your boat. The average person is lost, cut off, as it were. But if you really love, you don't need a boat. You go under the water.

Anyway it says something. Being apart is very painful and I am sure for you a great hardship. But you know it has deepened our relationship. Maybe "deepened" is not the best word. It has brought new life, strength, vision, examination, hope, dreams, sorrow, pain, appreciation, thanksgiving for what we have been blessed with. I love you. I love you. I love you with every muscle of strength I have.

My prayers go on each day and cry out for forgiveness for my own sins and those of my brothers. Sins of war, racism, injustice. I feel I have come to a sudden stop in my life and I have been stripped of everything I have ever been. I almost stand naked before the eyes of men, cheered by some, laughed at by others, pitied by others and admired by some. It is a strange feeling. Perhaps one feels what Christ must have felt like! I'll close here, bed-time, my love. Shalom to the children and to Casa.

Mike XXXX

Milwaukee County Jail-H-Annex
October 12, 1968   Saturday 9:45 p.m.

I love you forever!! My peaceful flowers: Shalom Netty, Willie, Brennan and Brigid,

Another day of separation (physically) from you has passed. But my spirit was and is with you every moment. I hope everything is fine at home Netty. As I was cleaning the cells today, plus doing my washing, I couldn't but think of all the work you have to do at Casa. I often wonder how you can do it, plus take care of the children. God is close to you Netty. He shines in your face. I am sure His Mother Mary is also present at Casa. We must always call upon Mary. She sure has known hardships also. Father Pat Flood came to see me. He is a beautiful man, said he would be getting in touch with you. It was good to see him. He lifted the spirits. Also Ed Walsh, S.J., came with Pat, great guy!! Sounds like a beautiful peaceful vigil tonight. Bless all those good people. We saw the Beatles on TV tonight in the movie, "Help." Very good, a fine break for us. Did you have time to watch?

I just opened Sacred Scripture and my eyes came upon these words. St. Mark, Chapter 10, verse 28: "Peter said to Him — 'Lo, we have left everything and followed you.' Jesus said, 'Truly, I say to you, there is no one who has left house or brothers or sisters or mother or father or children (or wife) or lands, for my sake and for the gospel, who will not receive a hundred-fold *now* in this time, houses and brothers and sisters and mothers and children and lands with persecutions, and in the age to come eternal life.'" I noticed He did not mention wife (I just put that in) but now that I read it again I can see why you never leave wife, only through death. You may be separated for a time, but you are always *one* together in spirit. Christ thought a lot about marriage, enough to change water into wine, enough to make it a sacrament. "What God has joined together let no man pull asunder." Enough to compare the sacrament of marriage with His own relationship with the Church or His mystical body here on earth. Meaning men who live up to his teachings here on earth. Netty, I have just been talking to Larry, sharing some of our thoughts. He really is a beautiful man. A man of great sensitivity. You know Netty, though these are painful times for all of us, I believe also that they are a blessing. A quote from Father Dan comes to mind: "It was not evil that was purified on Calvary, but goodness." I look upon these days in Jail as an opportunity to purify the good we have been doing up to now. Our marriage, our work at Casa, etc. We have been married for four years. And you know I have grown closer to you during all four years. I have had a chance to think and pray. My love for you has become as pure as the sun!!

Could you send me the *New Dutch Catechism* and *Prayers,* by Mike Quoist? I want to write something on marriage. My love reaches out to you and the children.

Shalom,

Mike XXXX

Milwaukee County Jail-H-Annex 4th Floor
October 13, 1968   9:30 p.m.
Sunday — 19th Sunday after Pentecost

My peaceful flowers, you are all as bright as the sun. I love you, Netty — Momma flower, Willie strong flower, Brennan strong flower and Brigid most beautiful flower — I love you, from Daddy flower.

A wee poem from somewhere:

"Climb the mountains and get their good tidings.
Nature's peace will flow into you as sunshine into trees.
The winds will blow their own freshness into you.

And the storms their energy, while cares will drop off
Like autumn leaves."

Beautiful is it not — sure is!! I read it today and thought it beautiful. So, I just had to share it with you my love.

This was a good day. I started reading the life of St. Francis by Kazantzakis. Really great and meaningful!! I should have a quote from that tomorrow. Tomorrow is a big day for the rest of the fellows. I hope there will be good news. I guess you saw the cartoon this morning in the Journal. Something else!!!! Some beautiful people came this morning and sang songs outside the jail, on the sidewalk. Their voices were like angels. Their song was like spring rain. Will close here, have to go to bed, lights out, my love to everyone. Kiss the children for me, tell them I love them very much and please God, I will be home soon.

Shalom,

Mike XXXX

Milwaukee County Jail-H-Annex
Written by the light of the bathroom
October 14, 1968   10:30 p.m.

My love Netty, Willie, Brennan, and Brigid,

I wanted to write something about our wedding ring. I just can't find words, but I mean to say I love you with all the spirit that my mind, soul and body can muster up!! You are my will, my flesh, my future, my joy, my sorrow, my pain, my spirit, my hope, my dream, my everything. You have brought me closer to God, more than any other person in my life to now. These days are sure strange and mysterious days. They have made me look very deep into myself, almost as deep as my very bowels. Searching for answers to *Why* questions and *What Reason* questions — Why wasn't I left alone, God, to my family and the work I had chosen? So few answers but a great peace and an assurance I was and am right!!

This experience is a sign from God our Father, I am sure of that. For years I have roamed homeless as it were — until I met you — over the earth; perhaps, I was searching for God. And now for the second time — the first was when I met and fell in love with you — I feel I am lying under a beautiful blossoming tree, with God blowing over me like a soft fragrant breeze. In the beginning, Netty, I was so afraid and very fearful — on both occasions — not knowing what was in store for me. I just had to jump, jump as it were, into the abyss. On both occasions, I have just done that and as a result a great beauty has been revealed to

me. And a great calm has come upon my waters. To use St. Francis'
words, Netty, "I am cold, I am hungry, I have nowhere to lay my head,"
until I found you, Netty. Oh, I want so desperately to open and share
my life with you, Netty, like never before. I am going to do just that.
For too long I almost took you for granted. At this point I don't want to
write to anyone — except short notes — until I first share everything of
myself with you!!

They just turned out the bath light, so I will try and continue by
the light of the hall light, which is dim!

My love, my love, my love, one thing I am beginning to really understand. God our Father is within us. Otherwise, we just could not
withstand being locked up behind these bars. We must not be afraid of
the look inward and obey the commands we are given there. Then and
only then will we find peace. After we find that peace, the bars don't
exist anymore for us. I believe that is what is happening to me. Don't get
me wrong. I am not yet without fear, but I am less fearful than I was.
Gandhi said the only way to peace is *peace* itself. I am beginning to
understand what he meant. *Peace,* he also said, is another word for God
as *truth* is. The abyss is within also, and our job as humans is to have
the courage to look closely at ourselves and then share what we see with
others. You are the one I want to share with most deeply. I love you
more than I could ever know. You are my every flesh and spirit. I am going
to stop here since my eyes are growing dim, though my hand wants to
continue. I will write more tomorrow morning. It is now about 12 p.m.
or so. I'll give you this on your visit, for you alone, and children, Netty.
I love you. Sleep peacefully my darling!!! X

October 15, 1968, 10 a.m.

Well, Netty, today everyone is in court except myself. So everything is rather quiet around here. A chance for me to sing the Psalms
and the office plus a rosary. And now an opportunity to say a few words
to you, my love. I heard and read in the paper this morning the courtroom scene last afternoon was a sight to behold. Looks like the trials
ahead are going to be newsworthy!! I don't know for sure what stage
I am at. Just hope this desert experience soon ends. I need your touch
and our love-making together. Oh, my gentle love. Each night here
for the last fourteen, we have had an extended biography of every one.
Really some great insights into these fellows. It sure is a privilege to
know these guys. Don Cotton just came back from court and his face
is shining. The bail for him is reduced down to $5.00. Great. We will
be out soon. This is the first glimpse of hope!! We must continue to pray.
God will soon answer our prayer. I'll close here Netty, until I see you

157

this afternoon. I love you. Give my regards to all at home. I just found out I go to court.

Love, Peace, Joy

Mike XXXX

Milwaukee County Jail-H-Annex
October 15, 1968 9:30 p.m.

My dearest Netty, Willie, Brennan and Brigid,

Today, what a day! Seeing you was more important than the entire court hearing. Well, at least, my chances of being with you soon are better. I love you, Netty, more than I ever could have imagined. This prison experience has been a sobering experience. It probably will be a great milestone in the deepening of our love. You mean more to me, Netty, than the world could ever give me. I am not just saying this from jail. You are so much a part of my flesh and spirit. It is unbelievable!! I love you very deeply!!

Getting out in the breeze and sunshine today was a great cause to be thankful. One learns in jail to be thankful for the smallest things. You become stripped of everything. Even your name. You are a number and when you are called by your first name, you are grateful. I am thankful for the food, air, my bed, books, water, rosary beads, and breviary, and letters from you and friends. My friends here, also. I am thankful for you and the children. For you, because you love and you back me when I have asked so much of you, for my lawyers, for those who vigil each night, for the community of support, for those who bring me food, for the nice guards, for Mass on Sundays. So many things!! I love you. I'll close here, praying for you for a beautiful tomorrow. I wish the children good night. My love Shalom.

Mike XXXX

Milwaukee County Jail-H-Annex
October 16, 1968 9:30 p.m.

My beautiful family I love you, I love you, I love you, I love you,

Today, I was hopeful for release, but I guess you are having some problems on the outside with bail and all that. I well understand. I am sure getting the bail together is a hard job. Anyway, I am hopeful for tomorrow. We have decided to let Basil and myself leave tomorrow if it can be arranged with our lawyer and you on the outside??

Something beautiful happened today. Father Pat Flood and Father Ed Walsh, S.J., came and had Mass with us, right in our cell. Really wonderful and a great cause for joy. Brought us all great peace!! I am most grateful. With all the expectation of getting out, one tends to feel very uneasy. That's me!! I love you, Netty, and I long for your tenderness and for us to touch without people watching or setting time limits on us.

My reflections today are about the poor, who never have enough money to be bailed out before they are tried. We are beginning to feel a little like them. Here we are nearly a month in Jail. And no bail yet. Of course, the poor don't even have defense committees set up for them. Thank God for all of you. We are mixing with other prisoners now. I see some of the fellows who come to the house to eat. Strange, isn't it? I almost have become one of them. I close here, looking forward to tomorrow for new hope. My love, my stretched-out hands. I long for you and your embrace.

Shalom,

Mike XXXX

Milwaukee County Jail-H-Annex
October 17, 1968, 10:10 p.m.

My love, Netty, and my dearest Willie, Brennan, and Brigid,

No need to tell you the *Joy* and anticipation in my heart tonight. Receiving the news from Mr. Jim Shellow today was some of the greatest news I have heard for a long time. I pray that everything goes well and I am sure it will. Just think of it, we will be together tomorrow. A time to talk and a time to make love. Yes, *make love,* now that is where it's at! I love you Netty, I love you, and I am going to take advantage of every chance to show you. I love you all so much!!!

A journey of men from exile
All with hands outstretched
Outstretched to greet their loved ones
Outstretched to embrace those they love.
Outstretched to fold and make love
With their dearest one
Outstretched in thanksgiving for
Once more being free.
Outstretched praising their Father
Outstretched hoping never to have to return to exile again!

Mike C.

159

"You must love the crust of the earth on which you dwell. You must be able to extract nutriment out of a sandheap. You must have so good an appetite as this, else you will live in vain." Thoreau.

Thought I would write that beautiful and meaningful quote to you. I entered jail, Netty, with eyes cast down, but in my despair, I discovered myself as it were, almost for the first time. Now I enjoy a new peace and a new joy and a new love. A gateway to a new future for me has been opened and I have been thrust through it, never to return through it again, despite my fears and inadequacies.

My love, my love, Shalom, until we meet on the morrow.

Mike XXXX forever

CHAPTER NINE

When we got out, thank God, after a month, we went back to our work, to the task of feeding hungry people, to the task of making our community more human, and because I felt responsible before the country and before my Creator, before God, to the task of telling people why I did what I did. That's why I spoke all over the country and I responded to whatever demands the courts or the law has made upon me in this past year.

But I didn't want to go out to the community immediately. Already in jail the question of hiring a lawyer became an intense issue. Should there be one lawyer for the 14?

I felt I had to have a lawyer, a local man, immediately. My case, because I had not waited quite long enough before the action to become a citizen of the United States, was different, special. I had to have someone to explain my position to go though all the implications of what I had done. I had to think of more than Mike Cullen, more than the lives of the 14. I had Netty and Willie and Brennan and Brigid to think about.

This decision was most difficult because suddenly I stood alone, even from the other thirteen. A further separation occurred because at this point I wasn't interested in proving legal things. I wasn't even interested in being political. I wasn't interested in going out and talking to people. I was still very overwhelmed by the action and the rawness of it and the death of it.

I was more interested in being with my family. I stayed in hiding for about five days and then I went out to the woods with my children,

161

just to be with them. To be alive was the most precious thing in my mind. I knew how much suffering Netty had gone through in the past month and I wasn't interested in having her go through more. I wanted to be with her, away from the house.

Casa was, after all, still a hot house. The place was still the scene of a lot of harrassment. It was so vulnerable, so open to any infiltrators. The action had been talked about all over the country. It was a national action — actually an international action. I do not deny that I was afraid, of course. I do not deny it. I was hesitant to speak for a while because I was sure the jail sentence would already be far too long. Shellow spoke to me most realistically, telling me all the implications and possible ramifications — how many years I might be in for. My one month in jail had taken away all naive notions of what prison is really all about. Our action was on top of the totem pole around the country. We had to be made examples. We could in no way expect mercy.

The prison sentence might have come very soon, showing the government's quick and decisive movement against un-American activities. So I wanted to spend as much time as possible with my family.

Gradually, when I knew it was going to be a long time before the trial, I also knew that my work could not wait. I began living a life again and a lot of new ideas began developing.

Father Larry Rosebaugh began full time to develop the Living Room, a place for the Skid Row men, the State Street men, to come and spend the night.

Frank Miller began developing an idea for a bookstore and soon the Rhubarb opened. The bookstore was to be a center for radical education, not just from the books housed there, but from meetings and discussions held there. It was taking Peter Maurin's ideas about round-table discussions a little further, a kind of free university, or a university of the streets. We also did draft counselling there. Bob Graf was especially involved in that. Art Heitzer eventually took over the store.

We began developing the idea for a school, a pre-school program for education. Before long we were serving some twenty-two children in an experimental, Montessori-like school, with voluntary teachers who were well trained.

The idea in all these ventures was to create alternatives to poverty, to find new ways. The action was a way to say no to the system, to its priorities, to its way of doing things. But we felt we should also be looking for alternatives, for better ways. Sometimes people have to say no without any other answers — at those times when immorality is so gross and rampant that immediacy is demanded. But we must never stop searching, probing, prodding, digging, experimenting, or we, too, stand condemned.

We became very serious about our publication, "The Catholic Radical." We had begun much earlier to publish a "sheet" called "Casa Maria Cry" which for the most part was no more than notes on the house, especially concerning needs and events and personalities. But we began to get more political, more aware of the world scene, more concerned about the war, the U.S. military machine, etc.

We were questioning things and our roots were Catholic. We felt if the Church was to be more involved, a paper was needed to get more into the roots of things. The underground press was communication to millions of young, mostly to the disenchanted. Couldn't there be one Christian voice speaking to those people?

We didn't think of "The Catholic Radical" as a division of the "National Catholic Reporter" or even of "The Catholic Worker," even though our roots are basically in Dorothy Day and her vision. I understand, for example, that originally "The Catholic Worker" was to be called "The Catholic Radical," but because Dorothy was a former communist and the communist paper was called "The Daily Worker," Dorothy's paper came to be called "The Catholic Worker."

"The Catholic Radical" hoped to get deep into non-violence, based on the Gospels. It tried to be an outlet for radical Christians. Father Dan Berrigan wrote one of the first articles and Father Jim Groppi wrote for us. It was bringing the life-style of radical Christians to the attention of more people. It became a record of where we had been and where we were trying to go. It helped us develop our thoughts, our expression, and became a gauge of our work in the community. The paper was also invitational, showing people our openness to their help and suggestions, inviting them to look at their lives and to see if they could relate to us. People did respond, many of them financially, to our invitation.

We published about eight times one year, a tabloid of various sizes, and we distributed as many as ten thousand copies. Joan Giehl, our dear friend, did the magnificent artwork. Ron Kramer, a young graduate of St. Joseph's College in Rensselaer, Indiana, became very involved with it. Then Father Norm Frederick, a Milwaukee archdiocesan priest who came to live with us, a very warm and wonderful Christian who did so much for us all at Casa, took the paper pretty much in his hands and did a great job with it.

The other important activity, the most basic and important one, that of feeding the hungry became greatly increased at this time. More people were stopping in at our house on twenty-first street, hungry people. Down the street from us the Highland Community Church had been vacant for over a year. The people who "owned" that church had tried to use it for various programs, but for the most part, the building was unused|. So we looked into the possibility of using the basement of the

163

church which had kitchen and dining facilities. We began having meals twice a week, and before long it became evident that we had to provide a meal every night. Over a hundred men were coming there to eat.

Now by this time seven "community" houses were in the immediate area and each house was responsible for preparing the begged food one evening a week. The food came from all parts of the city and from people of all faiths. Some months later the church trustees voted that we had to move out because of some tax law and so "The Meal" moved to St. Michael's a few blocks away.

The Casa Maria "community" is a vague kind of term to include all those people and all those projects that somehow were inspired by and/or were connected with Casa, all the people who began to feel a part of that way of life, a new way of life, not fully developed by any means, but experimental, innovative. We were a community but not a corporation. Each project was to be separate and totally self-supporting. In one sense we were really just part of the Catholic Worker movement, although that, too, is loose and flexible. It means being modeled after the philosophy of Peter Maurin, living the kind of life Catholic workers have known — not just being social workers or people who supply money. We must be literally there, bodily there. We must live it. We cannot come from the outside and permeate it. We may go out to speak, but we come back to our way of life. It becomes a whole way of life.

Somehow, although it is difficult to put into words, this kind of commitment demands deep resources. Some of the "community" houses were purely experimental in nature. Some of them did not buy the Christianity thing at all. One group went into a period of Mao and Marxist analysis. After a year this group broke up. I mean no condemnation, but when the weights of society came down on them, when the pressures were great, these people found nothing to fall back on.

I was never really afraid. I never worried about whether the city would come down on us with all it had on the books. I figured that as long as we were doing the right thing, we would succeed.

That's what I believe the gift of the Church is, that the Church is able to withstand mysteriously all kinds of pressures — even death. Even though the power of evil, the power of the state, tries to wipe you out, and even though at times it appears as if evil is going to win, faith tells the Christian that life will win — that life will win!

I'm not saying that we can expect people to accept the Christian faith, even if they were baptized into it. Faith cannot be imposed upon anyone. It is a gift. It is a sign that life will endure, an invitation to begin to live, a courage not to fear to lose everything, a stepping down to beginnings. Faith tells us not to be afraid of uncertainties.

Many people came to us to help, but often they did not come to grips with things, with life as it is. Often young people came with romantic notions of helping the poor and of establishing the ideal community. But there is a hard reality. Dealing with the down-trodden is not neat and easy. It means hard work. It means money is needed. In no way is it an escape or copping out.

The Gospels teach us the way. They bring us back to equality, they destroy racism and classism. They do not permit the scholar to look down on the worker, nor the worker to look down on the scholar. The Gospels demand that we meet one another as brothers.

But the Gospels also teach us to pray and I want to keep emphasizing that more than anything. Prayer has kept me going. Many times I've had to pray alone because I've found that most of our young people have been turned off by the Church because of its hypocrisy, or because of its silence in the face of so many and so important issues — issues important to their future like war and affluence and poverty. They've been turned off by everything in the Church, so they don't go to Mass, they don't pray.

But I know they are starving. Pot, the drug scene is one example of their poverty. Another example is the running and searching for new ideologies. Running for Marx — not that I'm totally against Marx, but running for Marx as a Savior. Running to the Red Book instead of the Bible. Running to Eastern thought as the only way to salvation and the future. Not that I'm against these things. They are very rich and we have to understand Zen so that we can understand ourselves better.

And so I have found it most difficult to call people to prayer. For a long time a priest came to offer Mass in my home but after a while I felt I was imposing it on the people there. I could not demand people to pray. I refused to do that. Many would not go to Mass on Sunday but would have their own form of service. OK. Better than being hypocritical and going to Mass even though they did not believe.

So many times I prayed alone, the Psalms and other prayers, the Breviary. How I would welcome the Eucharist, breaking bread, truly celebrating the meal of the body of Christ! The mystery, to share the mystery, that was my primary joy.

Not that we don't ask questions. We have to ask questions about marriage. What does it mean to be married? Netty was getting deep into the women's lib thing and I began to realize that I had to look at her differently than the typical Irish husband had done. I knew that if we couldn't be truly open to one another, we could not be truly married. We had to be open about all the things that are in our minds and in our spirits and in our feelings about other people and our relationships with other people.

165

The sign, the sacrament of marriage, is much deeper than the vows themselves, much deeper than the paper they are written on. They go deep into the marrow of the couple's bones, into the very depth of their being. That's marriage and I think we'll be strengthened by that. For that I knew I could go to jail and know our marriage would not die but would be strengthened, perhaps with new directions and new forms.

The Church, too, must continue to take new directions and forms. Like Bishop Buswell who came to the trial and testified, who came to Casa Maria and served food at tables, the Church must be a sign of love and concern for people, especially the poor. Its most visible sign must be among the poor. It doesn't mean that we are going to cut off all those rich young men in the world who want to become Christians. But the Church as sign must be with the poor. I'm hoping the Church has that courage.

I'm hoping the Church will always stand for human dignity, for the value of each man regardless of how inarticulate, how corrupted, how deranged. Feeding the poor — that's the most basic work for the Church, and until we do that we can't even speak of rehabilitation or renewal of any kind.

I'm hoping the Church will come alive on the Skid Rows of this country and elsewhere and will recognize, as one Skid Row man told me, that capitalism is fit for the garbage can of history.

I think that if Christ were born anywhere today, he would certainly be born on Skid Row. The Son of Man would be born there because this is the lowest place, the stable of society. Christ would be there because these men are on the bottom of the ladder, and where Christ is, there the Christian must be. Christians must choose this as a vocation, just as at times they must choose jail and even death.

The Church must have a respect and a gentleness for life. The love for life must show concern for every kind of person at every state and stage. It must recognize violence as the misuse of persons. The Church must see exploitation of persons as violence and that refusing to give anyone bread is violence.

The Casa Maria community, though all did not admit it or even want it to be the new Church, was certainly an example of what it could become. A Quaker family became a part of us. There were intellectuals and scholars with bricklayers. A Spanish family and an Indian family were a part of us. Peter Maurin used to speak about the scholar and the laborer working side by side, complementing each other, the scholar becoming a worker and the worker a scholar.

An experiment was also happening on a plot of land in Northern Wisconsin which we called the Thomas Merton Catholic Worker farm. We hoped that this could at least be the beginning of trying to understand what the land could offer as an alternative for some people. It was a kind of retreat house, a place to get away and to study, which I think is terribly necessary for any one of us who happen to be in the front lines of trying to launch new possibilities for the Church and the larger community. It was a retreat but also a place for hard work in the Benedictine tradition of "Prayer, Work, and Study."

Community houses began to develop on the East side of Milwaukee, also, and we began trying to bring our lives together and to share experiences.

So there were busy times after the jail experience. And in the midst of them, as time passed by waiting for the trial, I began to see that I was obligated before God and this country to tell people why I participated in the Milwaukee 14 action. The action had confused people, even though many of them could not justify their own silence regarding the war.

I had gone through a period when I couldn't go out and face audiences and talk about the action because it hadn't clarified itself in my own head, what it meant to me. But when I saw that people were more confused by the burning of paper than by napalming people, I began to travel and to speak.

This was very hard on Netty. It was like the beginning of the jail sentence. But I felt I was not the property of one person or persons or of one community. I was not married to just one person. I realized that my children were not just the possession of Netty and myself, but that they belonged to the community — just as anyone else's children were my responsibility.

Families give us a much closer view of what life's about, because if we realize how much we love our own children, this should teach us how much we should love every man, woman and child. What a world we would have! Isn't that what life's all about? That's the direction we must take — that the community must share — in sharing responsibility for all children, in forming food cooperatives etc. But people are all hung up on just their immediate family. This distortion stretches marriage into a totally different form. Rather than embrace all people and all children, it turns itself in on itself and this is the tragedy of marriage. Of course, a certain amount of privacy is necessary and a house with children must have a certain kind of natural rhythm in it simply because children need a kind of natural rhythm.

But I came to be less worried about Netty and the children, though the pain of separation in jail would be inconceivably great. The separation became painful immediately when I began my speaking tour.

The first invitation I accepted was in Peoria, Illinois. I brought to that talk everything I was. I knew that the action was not something separate from my feeding the hungry or running a Hospitality House.

167

It was very much in keeping with the works of mercy. It was very much in helping with what the Church was supposed to do.

This is what I told the three hundred in the audience that night. The press and the cameras were there and I couldn't believe that this thing was so important, that I was sort of a national figure with the people in the peace movement. My thoughts were not totally clear that night, but I said what I had to say with complete honesty and sincerity.

I told the audience they had to muster new ways of saying no to death. Whether a person was a journalist, a politician, a lawyer, a laborer, a student, anyone and everyone must begin to say no.

Peoria was a real experience for me. The response was tremendous, encouraging. One man stood up and heckled, but after the talk he came to me and we talked till 4:00 a.m. I was exhausted, but after one hour he called to say he couldn't sleep and to ask whether he could come to talk some more. He came and talked till morning and finally he said he had a business trip into Chicago and he'd give me a lift. When we got to Chicago he skipped his appointment and we talked some more. This man went back to Peoria and started working on tax resistance and I'm not sure what happened to him.

The experience convinced me I had to keep speaking and I traveled from Milwaukee to Kansas City to Denver, to Pueblo, to Washington D.C., to Baltimore, to New York, to Boston, to Pittsburgh, to Cleveland — to thirty-four states in all.

When I went to a college two or three days, I went not just to speak, not just to tell people about war and how radical I was, but to get to know the people that I went to see. I wanted to know their lives. I was touched more by them than I touched them. I learned more from the young people I spent nights rapping with than I taught them. We searched together for new solutions to the problems of history. We mustered our hope. We sang and danced together.

And this travel taught me great things about this country — that this is a rich land, this is a rare land; that this is a fresh land and a fair land. I began to believe that the young people of this country would not let a Hitler be reborn here, that we will never see a Dachau in America. There's lots of work ahead but a beginning has been made. Young people realize that America cannot be great because of its economic wealth, or its great armies, or its technological advances. We must become great because we are more a people than a nation. If we are more a nation than a people, we must and will be destroyed.

We know we have the power in this society in our time to murder every man, woman and child on the face of the earth at least four times, and that's not an abstraction. That's fact! But we have to be able to stand against that as a young people, as a people of faith, as a people of hope, and believe that the fact of peace can still withstand these times and we can grow and walk into the future.

This is the only reason that I would enjoy going to jail, that I knew going to jail was winning, because I knew that going to jail was moving us forward. No sacrifice is really enough, not even death, and I have thought much about death, that many of us, though not black like Fred Hampton, will be killed or murdered. Some of us in white skins will be murdered for being non-violent. But I believe that a non-violent minority can have a real position of power. I truly believe that the Christian today, Christians with a future are absolutely obligated to be non-violent.

But death must be faced, realizing that people may die in many forms and not just physically. Gandhi was much more alive after he was dead. He had great insight into this before he died. He welcomed death as a natural form, as being transformed. Martin Luther King, Jr., understood that death is redemptive, even though he and all of us want to live. Believe me, during those thirty days in jail I prayed to get out. I said, you let St. Paul out; now you've got to get me out. I'm sure I'd pray the same way if I were truly faced with death.

I love life. I like a good time. I'm no party pooper, I'll tell you that. I love songs and music and poetry and plays and movies and friends and people and good rapping sessions and light rapping sessions, and drinking a little, whiskey once in a while, good Irish whiskey, or a good beer.

(But because they demanded me to come to trial, I am here. I know why I am here. I know I'm here to tell you and to tell the Court and to tell the jury. I am not asking you an easy thing to do, whatever may be, either to acquit me or to send me to jail for whatever time.

Did I burn files? Yes, I did. Did I enter a draft board? Yes, I did. Did I do it with free will? Well, if you mean by free will, did anybody coerce me, no, no one coerced. But a free will? I am not sure. I would say this. I had to do what I did, lest we be mad, and lest we go insane as a society, as a people, as persons.

And I think that most of our young men who have gone off to prison have said the same thing, young men who have resisted the draft. Not that they haven't loved their country, but because they have loved their country, and knew they had to pay a price. The price in these days is not to be a soldier like in the past, but to be the soldier of the future. Men and women must be willing to come into a courtroom and to the jails of this society, to come in as we came in here, not treating the marshalls or the judge or the jury or the prosecution as our enemy, but seeing them as our brothers, and treating them as we would like to have them treat us, as brothers, and as sisters. I think that's the gift. That's an echo of a thousand years and a thousand beyond that. And that is an echo of the beginnings of this nation's history, you see.

These are strange times, hard times, tough times, but great times. Because we are here we are part of one another here. Maybe we are listening. Maybe we will have better politicians and better judges and juries, and a better understanding of what punishment means in terms of punishment as we see it carried out by some of our judges today and particularly by our jails. Our jails are not the best places they could be and maybe people like ourselves can point that out.

The others of the 14 are pointing this out to the State. Up in Waupun, many were put in the hole many times. In Fox Lake, Father Larry Rosebaugh was in the hole because he wrote an article for "The Catholic Radical" which I am primarily responsible for publishing. Again, radical means from the roots, trying to understand what the roots of being human is, particularly in relation to the Gospel.

And Catholic means universal, understanding the universality of the family of man and woman. Bob Graf is another who has suffered the hell of the hole. His wife came to visit him right before the birth of his son and he placed his hand on her stomach where new life was being lived and created. For that action he was brought in before a group of men who said that he would be put in the hole for three days for manhandling his wife. That is sick.

And so our jails have to be reformed. Many of our institutions have to be reformed. Our corporations in many ways have to be reformed. But you see, the task is not just for one of us. The task is for all of us. It's for you and for me. We must take on the responsibility of doing the best thing we know how to do. Though heavy and hard that may be, we must do the best thing and the right thing for us, for you and for me, for all that we know is in us, to be human, and that can only be answered by each person.

For the Christian, for the Catholic, that means, in traditional terms, that we must bear witness. I am not a theologian, but I have some notion of what that means.

When I was working at the Casa Maria, I used to take courses from Father Bernard Cooke at Marquette. The truth is that he used to let me sit in on his courses. One was on the liturgy, the most central service or celebration of the Christian community, the breaking of bread in memory of Jesus of Nazareth. I took a course on Sacraments, the signs of how God or how the Church can be most viable, of how God can be most visible through the signs of the Church in the world.

This is what God means to me. He is the sign of life, the sign of love in the world. Visible, even physical in the world. And the sacraments are external signs of the Church.

Father Quentin Quesnell, who teaches Scripture at Marquette, used to come to the house to give us his insights on the Old and New Testament, particularly the New. These insights were very important to me, and it became clearer to me what witness is. Primarily, witness is vocation. One of the three marks of the Christian community has traditionally been to bear witness. The Greek word is "Marteria." I believe that means to be a sign of the things that Christ sent us to do. For example, we must feed the hungry, perhaps one of the hardest things that Christ asked us to do. We can believe all the things in the Gospel and speak about them, but unless we feed our brothers and clothe our brothers and serve our brothers and be a peacemaker and stand for our brothers, we do not know what the faith is all about. You know, we can have all the grand churches and all the cathedrals across the world and they might be filled, but if the community doesn't feed the hungry, what are we as a church? We may have great political powers in the whole community, but what is that political power in the world community if we don't feed our brothers and stand up for our brothers when that brother or sister is being destroyed or being dehumanized or being betrayed?

So to witness is to stand on behalf of your brother or sister and, of course, it goes all the way to where Christ's life went, to the point of his death on a cross out of love for men. Nailed to a tree at thirty-three years of age. Chosen over Barrabas who was a revolutionary of his time. Christ, a man of peace. Murdered by Caesar's army. Nailed to a tree. Out of love rather than saying I can speak or I can run away or I will become revolutionary or I will take up violence. He would rather go to his death.

Some thought he was going to bring a new kingdom, set up a big church or something like that, a church like we have with all kinds of executives and so forth in it, but he didn't. He came to bring a new kind of kingdom, a kingdom that would be less clerical perhaps than the Jewish nation of his time had become, not bound to a lot of laws, but very human and very much into the community. This was to give us an idea of what eternal life is about beyond the grave, and to show us it is our task to work on behalf of the common good of all men and all women, to bear witness to the point of martyrdom, to be willing to give our own blood now as Jesus' own blood was spilled on Calvary rather than spill somebody else's. That to us is witness. And there are many degrees.

You bear witness here in this courtroom. Each one of you is trying to bear witness to what your conscience says. The judge must be true to his conscience. The jury must be true to their consciences. The jury must not be swayed by any one of us, by political harrassment or whatever it may be, but must be true to their consciences and willing to stand on behalf of their consciences. Or the prosecution. Or the guards. Or the marshals. Or the men who are here to protest our presence here and the court system. Being true to what we are is the most important thing.

Witness. It is a vocation. It has a degree of — what can I call it? Maybe some kind of degree of — I can't get a word. Calling. I don't know where it comes from except it is there. When I acted it is because it is in my bones, it is in my face, my hands, my feet, how I must act and how I must live. No one can understand fully except it is a gift and it is not just the person alone.

"Diakonia" is another word that comes from Greek. I guess the word deacon came from it. At any rate, the word means to serve, and it relates to witness. Service. Service of the poor is in essence what the command of Jesus is all about. To love your enemies and to serve your brother. The Christian may not see a man as an enemy, but must look deeper into a man and see him in the larger context of the family of man.

Evil can be made very visible, but in spite of the evil man commits, we must be able to see the human being who commits it. Otherwise we deny our own humanity.

So "Marteria" and "Diakonia" relate to one another. Witness is manifested through service, how I serve my brother and my sister in the family of man, how I serve the poor and the dispossessed and the old and the young and the most inarticulate and the most frail and the fearful, and the most ostracized by society, and the brothers who are born in black skin and have the same blood and the same pulse in their body as you and me, and the Chinese who have yellow skin and have the same blood and tears and hopes that you and I have.

The third mark of the Church is "Koinonia," a Greek word meaning fellowship, community. This is hard to explain except that I could never be here if it weren't for you. I could never be here alone. I could never be here if it weren't for Netty and for the many human beings and brothers and sisters whom I have met and with whom I have entangled my life and had fear with and tried to grow with and have been touched and healed by! If it weren't for Dorothy Day, if it weren't for Bishop Buswell, if it weren't for my father and mother. Community, too, is a mystery, a great gift. It comes from the Creator himself.

Why were we born? Why are we alive? What is our life about anyhow on the planet? What is the destiny of life itself? These are all questions to which I have no answers. The answers are great and magnificent mysteries, mysteries of creation. The fact of the sky being blue and the earth being green and the mountains being tall and snow-capped. And the fact of the smile of a child, and on and on, and the animals as they dance and live. These are tremendous things in life for which we

172

have no answer. But we will continue to grapple with the questions for centuries to come as men and women have grappled with the questions for centuries and for thousands of years already up to now.

But we are at a point in history and there are certain questions we must answer for the life of all of us, and they are truly related to poverty and the divisions among men and women along ideological and political lines. Once and for all these questions must be faced. Whether one believes in communism or democracy does not give that person a right to kill or to use napalm, because we are brothers and sisters of one family. To me that is the heart of where we are.

"Koinonia" is most exemplified when people get out of themselves to work out of love for one another. We don't set out to feed the hungry because we feel obliged to, but we are in love and we are thankful and we know it is a privilege to feed the hungry. Not because some day we might be hungry, but because they are our brothers and sisters and they belong to the same community of man. The early community of Christians sold everything as Christ asked his first friends, the Apostles to do. Tough demands! He said sell! Remember the rich man who came up to Jesus and asked what he had to do to gain eternal life. Christ told him to obey the Commandments, the Commandments which he knew: not to kill, and love the Lord your God with all your heart and soul and will, and love your neighbor as yourself, your brothers and sisters, all men and women as yourself. A tough job, not always agreeable. The young man said he had done all these things. Well, Christ said, if you want to do better, sell everything. Sell all that you have and come follow me. Now, that's a tough job. The man hung his head and turned around and walked away from Jesus.

I think these are hard things to ask people today, too, just as they were tough to ask 2,000 years ago. But if the distribution of the earth's resources, if the goods of the earth are to be equally shared by all men and women, if the goods of this society, if the land, for example, is to be divided and shared, a tough job awaits us, but perhaps a necessary job if we are to have a future.

When I was in Delano I saw clearly that the real victory of Caesar Chavez will come when the land owners, the grape growers, share their land with the poor, with the men and women who work in the fields and who have worked there for generations, the people whose blood and sweat lie deep beneath the soil of this country.

And the Indians must be free to walk the land and to live where they want, with more privilege perhaps than we have and certainly as much freedom. After all, these people were here before Columbus ever got here. These are tough things to ask of people, because we are afraid to render to

173

them lest we lose all that we have. But we must not be afraid of losing by giving people their due because in losing we gain.

How much freedom both Netty and myself have gained by selling almost everything! Oh, yes, we rely on people's goodness for bread and for food and on their friendship. But we know we are only at the beginning of our lives and we must begin to work for alternatives in this society. This means more than burning files, more than feeding hungry people.

We must work for alternatives like developing cooperatives, particularly among the poor in areas like medicine where the poor will get together to hire their doctors as a community. This would place responsibility on the poor themselves. They must see themselves that they can bargain as a group of people, and that mere monetary gain is not the way into the future. Making $10,000 doesn't make a person happy or $100,000 or $1,000,000. Many men and women who make that money are in despair. Our society is one big example of that. People who got very rich like the world has never seen before are not happy. But cooperating, working together is the greatest gift and the greatest need in history.

The small farmer, for example, is disappearing from our society. My wife grew up on her parents' farm in northern Wisconsin and she grew up with hard work in her early youth, just as I had in Ireland. And both of us have a great love for farming and for farmers and for the land. Many of the Europeans who came here were farmers, but the farmer has been displaced. Six per cent of the people of this country now are supplying the cities. But the cities are not real alternatives to men and women for a future. Our cities are terrible accidents, born out of an industrial society in Europe and carried on here. We find ourselves with polluted cities and inadequate transportation, and overcrowdedness and poverty and violence and what have you. And this has happened, I think, because we have never allowed the land to be an alternative. We are not an agrarian people, but perhaps we have to become one, if we are to make the city an alternative for us to live in in the future. I intend to spend all the days that I have to work and help that happen, to help make alternatives possible.

As we feel and see institutions, be they in the church or in the state, failing us and failing mankind and failing to meet the needs of these times, we must develop alternatives, be they educational institutions, be they political institutions, be they corporations, and on and on. We must develop alternatives that can speak to people and touch people's lives and make our lives whole and human.

For example, I would like to see cooperatives in the northern region of Wisconsin where the farmer is being displaced today because he can't make enough to live on, and so has to migrate to the city in order to get a job where he finds himself inarticulate and ill-prepared. Some of these men are in their forties and fifties and find themselves uneducated and unskilled and so are on the doles of society, on the Skid Rows or welfare roles, or unemployment roles. We must take the land and make it an alternative place to live for people so that we can stay human.

But we must keep speaking to the questions of war with all the humanity we know that we can muster. We must try to be that sign of hope. We must go on feeding the hungry. We must help develop food cooperatives, because the poor, you see, have been blinded just as much as any of us in the middle class have been blinded. They have been exposed to the same media, the same mentality. Money-making has been the goal and has been the sign of winning. But we have to change that value system.

The best example of this for me is Caesar Chavez. Martin Luther King was just beginning to see what would truly change and help the black community to become a full-grown community because he would have offered a new value to a middle class community. Profit making, money, home, suburbs, and all of that, are perhaps important but not worth emphasizing to the point of ignoring the real, human values of life. Chavez is not just asking the people of Delano to come out of the fields and to join the picket line, even though he's been on that picket line for four years. He's offering the people a new way of life. He has developed cooperatives, cooperative clinics, cooperative housing, credit unions, etc.)

To me that's real resistance; that's the real social change. This must be the direction of the future.

But my name is not Chavez. I am not a product of his part of his history. I was born at a different time and at a different place and I was chosen to point in another direction concerning another major need in our society. So I burned files. Why?

(I guess it was because I felt there was nothing else left to do. Of course we had lots of people to feed. I had seen the dreaded barbed wire in Chicago. I saw the direction in which society was headed. I had seen our cities burning and the misplaced priorities of this society and a foreign policy that was not changing. I felt we were being betrayed.

And so we had to speak to the community as loudly and as humbly as we could begin to speak. The best way I knew how was to show people that we were serious, that we were not joking. We had to speak with all that was in us, bringing our own lives in jeopardy, our own future and the future of our people, of our community, of our families. And so we decided to speak and to stand and to wait for arrest — wait for society to come for us.

But what was evident was that most people, because of the law or because of our value system that has developed over many years, find themselves on the side of burning human beings rather than on the side of burning paper. That's a tough thing to understand.

I didn't expect the action to end the war. I expected Americans and brothers and sisters of the community I was living in to examine their lives as best they knew how, and to begin to respond as best they knew how in the future. That's why I spent the last year all over the country, talking, sharing with people what I felt. I shared with all the truthfulness and honesty in my bones and in my mind. The details I'm not afraid to talk about, and I hope that you will be different tomorrow than today and that you will become more American in the full sense of the word by being more human. I hope you will develop those great freedoms we have and that are truly ours because we live in this land.

All I know is I did what I did lest I be judged not a man but a coward. I did what I did even though I knew I jeopardized my wife's future and the future of my children. I did what I did even though I jeopardized a future in this society. But I stood with those other men on that day, on that evening, in that place, and at that time, lest I be judged less a man. I did it lest I be condemned. And so I stand before you. So God help me!

CHAPTER TEN

May 15, 1970. The scene was familiar — the federal building in Milwaukee. The young people and other friends began to gather about an hour before the 11:00 a.m. opening of court.

The whole scene brought me back to the wild week of the trial — the courtroom packed each day, the marvelous liturgies and celebrations we had each night, the friendship and community that formed with people all over the country, and especially the fantastic Mass we celebrated at midnight, a few minutes after I was declared "guilty" — sharing the Eucharist on the very spot, the triangle, where the files were burned.

I had been convicted on two counts of burning draft records and of interfering with the administration of the Selective Service. Potentially, the sentence could have destroyed me, but because of the comparatively light sentences of the other thirteen, I was truly hopeful that I would get no more than two years.

A dozen clergy, many young people, and, just as during the trial, Netty and the children were present. I asked Judge Gordon whether I could speak before the sentence was pronounced.

I told the people in the courtroom, especially the young people, that they must be about a better America. I told them the hour was late and dark, that they should take the times seriously, that they needed to be disciplined, that this was no time for sporadic violence. I urged the young people to become real students, to study, to develop a theory on how to bring about a new human world.

"America, in my mind," I said, "is no lie, and it was not intended to be a lie by our forefathers. But it has been betrayed.

177

"You must be serious, you must be disciplined, and above all, you must be non-violent."

I then requested that I be able to take a few books with me to prison.

Jim Shellow told the judge that the community would gain little by my imprisonment and that he was sure it would gain much by my freedom. He cited some historical precedent.

Judge Gordon was very kind. He told the court that the defendant had some "commendable characteristics," but that he had committed a crime and must be punished — especially since he was a recognized leader of the action. For these reasons, he said, he was sentencing the defendant to one year and a day, that he could sentence him to no more and no less.

The year and a day was a favor in the sense that by being longer than a year, I *could* be eligible for parole after four months. I requested that my sentence begin immediately, put a stack of books under my arm, flashed the peace sign to all, and left for jail.

I headed for the door. The full courtroom was very quiet. Then I heard the voices of my sons, Willie and Brennan.

"Good-bye, Daddy."

"Bye, Daddy."

Epilogue

Michael Denis Cullen was refused parole, but by work and good conduct, he was released from Sandstone Federal Penitentiary, Sandstone, Minnesota, on February 12, 1971. After nine months in prison and a year on a farm in northern Wisconsin, Michael and Netty and their three children are now living on the second floor of an old apartment building near the edge of an urban renewal project in the inner city of Milwaukee.

The U.S. Immigration Service started deportation action against Michael in April, 1972. At this printing, hearings have not yet been held.

Appendix

My God
12:15
A journey from Milwaukee to Madison
A house whose people I hardly know
Their daughter who spent some days with us
A room by myself
A book and some tapes
A book by Dan
Dan Berrigan

Some pages I've read
And in my guts lies something
I don't know what it is
I just need to explode
But it must come out
That I'm sure of
I'm not sure quite what it is
But it must come out in order that I might sleep

What is it
Many things I am sure
It's the thoughts of a son of mine Brennan who is sick
Whom I've just been alerted by phone this morning as to his sickness
It's Netty my wife
Whom I know has walked too many painful roads

The burning light of love
Of good future
Is almost out
At least the wick has been burnt down too low
She cries out for hope
She cries out for someone to hold on to her
To help her through whatever course we are on

It's the thoughts about what I've begun
What I've started to carve
Make the Casa
Its work-people-faces
The human faces of the men
The many who come
The many who have passed on

The Tates and the Eds and the Hermans
Tate
Tate the singer
Lonely man
Talking guitar
Ed
In his proud blackness
And his wondering vision
Whose color never existed

The love-ones
The dancing people of eternity
The lives of men and women I've touched these past few weeks
Who, because of what they are
Beautifulness
Gentleness
Loneliness
Cling to the very belly of my soul

And the empty barren world
Buried in its own hypocrisy
In its own
I don't know

Words
Jungle dust
Always words

Saying so little to anyone who could listen
But are my life at this time

I speak
I speak
I speak like I have been filled with something I've hardly under-
    standing of
It's pushing out of my body
To be taped
To be written
To be something
To be shown
To be presented

What I am saying really are my fears
Fantastic at this time
That weigh me down to the ground
They cling in every muscle and every fiber of my soul
They burn in my skull

And I am alone
On some bloody hill somewhere
I say bloody because there's nothing around
Except the fragrant smell of beautiful memories
Everything that I have done has been buried
Like falling leaves upon a winter's evening
From trees that have become so bare
They are almost dead

This night is a canvas
My soul the palate
My words the brush
And I must paint
That one thing I am sure of
I must paint

I must take my brushes and speak
A journey into searching
That I could never have dreamed was possible
How in my own so many inabilities
Could have dared to be invited
But I have been invited

It's now my responsibility to tell
To speak to talk to tell you
To make visible the journey
The exile
The desert
The lonely hill
The burning sky

From a jailhouse which was desert
And yet Spring
With flowers
And trees
And lovely skies
And sunshine
And sand and pebbles
And water
And rainbows
Into something that was despair

Another time
Court-City-Problems
Lonely faces empty bellies drunken men crying children shouting voices
Lonely wife
Tender touching hand
How could this make sense to anybody who could hear it
For me I will not know what
I have no idea how it will turn out
It's been hard times lately for me
In my own self

Ah friends
Friends whom I could write for
Describe where I'm at
The confusion
The despair
And yet the joy

I dance sometimes in my spirit
I dance and I sing
Because yet the loneliness
The sorrow
In a sense is really much liberating
Strange isn't it

The assurance
The assurance of something new
Of something very good

The revolution is within me
As the Kingdom of God is within us
The struggle is within me
Between self and the kingdom

Within ourselves
That's what it is
Molding
Stripping
Tearing apart tearing off
Layer by layer
Our mortal selfs
To become new men without fear
With vision
With great joy
With a newness that burns the earth
That fills the darkness
A torch with ever-lasting fire

That's where it's at
That's where it's at
That's where I know it's at

Madison
Staying at this house
Family Kathy was over at our house
Me taping into a microphone
Hoping to write it down at some later date
So much to tell
Sometimes I think there's not much to tell
But there is so much to tell

The human story
A journey
A little home in Ireland
Town of Wicklow
Through Roscrea and County Tipperary
Throughout Ireland to Knock and Mayo
Knock a small little town

Mayo — meant a lot to me
From Scotland to England
Lockbury London New York
Colorado Missouri Wisconsin
Then Georgia and all these places
Through an insurance agency
Getting married
Having children — three of them now
To starting a hospitality house for the poor

From Casa Maria
To the faces of thousands
That came and went in three years
Touching each one of them
Touching us
To tell the story now
Of who they are
And what they have done for me

And why
Because I keep touching something
Beautiful things
Some beautiful people
Some beautiful fires
That don't singe my hand or my hair
But make my hand an invisible shining glowing
My soul
At oneness with my flesh
My spirit
Rhythm
Moving dancing singing

That's why
That's what I'm saying
In a song
In a paper I might write
In this tape tonight
In the making of love
In dancing

Can I go to sleep yet
No
My spirit refuses to let me sleep yet

From the fasting at the Cathedral
Fasting and standing at the federal building
From saying no to war so many times
To the burning of some draft files
The jail cell of the county of Milwaukee
To getting out
Press people question asking
And the talks public appearances
Loneliness
The deadliness in the after of it all

Now to reconstruction
Rebuilding of a community
Not so much rebuilding as redirection
The strain of starting a new school

To Netty
Who is having a hard time
Who I must help
In every sense and being I have

To everything

It's almost like we're mad
Drunk perhaps is a better word
Drunk with what we are trying to express
Drunk with the love that burned our lives
That made us reach out to every man
To every woman and child to say I love you
I need you
You are me
You are myself

You black man
You poor man with no food in your belly
You child who is crying
You son of mine
You wife
You bishop
You father
You
You
You whoever you are

You burning baby with napalm
You starving Biafran
You Latin American
You who is the center of the jungle
You my brother
You I love
You I tell you
You I must share
You
You I love

I am the accumulation of the touch of every man I have met
And woman and child
They have been so beautiful
So sorrow-ridden
So torn
So shiny-faces
So laughing, so smiling
So up-tight
So sincere
So corrupt
So naked
So business-like
It's impossible to go on at this time
I am a result of their presence in my life
Ah what a thing
What a beautiful thing

Tonight
I played back a tape of Tate
Made at the house last summer
That was this man from the road
Who came to Casa for a while
Spent a month or so
Was an alcoholic
Twenty-six
Bitter ex-army
Who had a guitar and his clothes
And himself
That was all he had
But God had he so much
He cried out to me in a sense in his songs

I think of all the beautiful people we meet in life
That we never touch
We never even dare to get to know
If we would we would never kill a man
We would never think of taking arms
Anytime anywhere
We would never harm a person through speaking against him
Maiming him with our words
Words that would outkill the guns
Destroying character
As we often do in our society

And I think we must all get to this way
We must listen more to every person
To hold them
As if they were the most sacred thing created
As if they were God
Perhaps they are

Each person
Sense-sensitivity
Part of me
I love you
I love you I love you I love you I love you
These are the only words I have
These are the only words I would live and die for

I love you life
I love you dancing rainbow
And crying child
I love you young man
Who is within the jail
Or without on the street
Who is surrounded in black skin or brown
Who has a starving belly
Or very little joy for Christmas
Who has many children and no head
Who is Brennan with his own personality at one and a half years of age
Who is Willy smarter than most his age
Who are Netty's parents
Good good oh so good
Farmers good people

I love you Netty
I love you
I love you
I love you Netty more than the word can carry
More than I could dream or say
The more I feel
In my soul in my flesh in my marrow
In the depths of my bones I love you
I love you I love you I love you

Dance you rainbows
Sing you skies
Shout from the mountains
The waters flowing forever into the tides of the time
Screaming out to men of history
Screaming out to every soul
Screaming it out I love you
I love you I love you I love you I love you I love you

I love you policeman
I love you because you don't understand what it's all about
So you are forced to carry a gun
I love you soldier
Oh soldier in battle
Burnt too by napalm
Created by your own brothers
In a land you think you are protecting

I love you dying child
Burnt by that napalm
I love you mother
I love you Vietcong Vietnamese
Trying to protect the soil
The future
I love you

I love you with tears of pain
But I love you
I love you in the mistakes of myself
In the sins I have committed
Consciously or unconsciously
In being negligent fearful selfish I love you
Forgive me for not being so good

As good as I should be really
I ask you forgiveness for not being so good
As conscious as I should be

I love you Dan Berrigan
For being so courageous
So rich and beautiful
I love you Father Groppi
For helping all of us know ourselves
I love you each man each woman each child who comes to Casa
Sam you're a good man
You are beautiful in your blackness
Color will never matter again
You are my friend companion support
You brought me to myself
To you I was as a white man
In a world deadly with white people
Herman my friend I love you
In the streets of state street
From the streets
Of the streets of the country
A hobo they call you Herman love you
Mary Jo
Mary Jo I can't make words up
And Kathy and Dan
And Father Larry smarter than any of us
And Bob and John
And all the household
And all my friends of the Milwaukee 14
I love you
I love you
I love you

I am asking forgiveness
For not being such a man
When I should be a man
For being confused
When I should be stable
For being selfish
When I should be less selfish
For being rough
When I should be gentle
For not being there

When I should be
Forgiveness is the word

Jesus called it confession
Called it penance
Absolution absolve
Absolve me from my sins
Absolve
And thank you for your greatness
For your tolerance
I love you

Love
Love Dan called it at the end
I call it flowers
I see lots of them — lots
Whirling winds teasing us
Flipping us like pebbles on the ocean floor
Weighing down us sometimes
And yet picking us up letting us float
As if we were just the air itself
I love you

I call it dancing rainbows
Bright sky
Laughter singing and dancing
Rhythm
Freedom liberation
Gift of gold frankincense and myrrh
Burning fire
Burning burning burning fire
Burning like it consumes the earth
And man
Carrying him into the eternity of everything

Father forgive us
And help us continue to know and to love
To dance and to sing
To be at peace and to give peace
To be justice and to carry out justice
I love you
Price we must not talk of
We must go on loving

Loving feeding clothing sheltering
Standing up when we should
Being disciplined in some way
Always seeking out
Knowing when to stop
Knowing where we must take a breath
And happy to know
Being a sign of hope

God I love you
I love you the word is love
LOVE
Love-stretching out our hands to every man
Holding on touching
Touching
And lifting
Being there when sorrow strikes closest
Laughing when we should laugh
Making a chain to circle the world
Until there is no more space for anyone
Nothing else to be seen except men who are chained together
Or dancing together
Or singing
Or forever one-one in love
Love
Love man's purpose
Love man's meaning
Love man's destiny

Jesus said
The Kingdom of Heaven
I will give you the Kingdom of Heaven
Tell the world of the news
Tell man he must not fight again
That he doesn't have to fight

Herman my friend said we must be kind to one another
Love your neighbor as your brother
That's it
That's where it's at
Love each man each woman each child
As if they were and are a part of your own flesh
Your own person

Your own spirit
Your own bone
I love you

No more wars
No more empty bellies
No more uneducated
No more cold
But concern
By work
By being part
Everybody as we can be
By being example
By going on
By having faith and courage
Being gifted
I love you I love you I love you

I must stop
My spirit is dancing — and I must stop
I just love you
It's so beautiful
To be able to say these things in so many ways
Though whoever may not understand them
It's so great to be free enough to say them
To say what's moving within our souls
It's so beautiful
So peace giving or something
Because when they are said something is lifted from our shoulders
A journey into the snow country of the north tomorrow
I must stop here

God
Thank you for this opportunity
Thank you for the sights you have shown me
A world that I never knew could have existed
Such as background I only have had
And yet you have chosen us
Among the fishermen
Among the tax-collectors
Among the uneducated
You've chosen us to show to see
What you have built for us

193

And to tell the world about it
The vision
The new Jerusalem the new city
About yourself
Father

Father
Our Creator our Lover
Our Friend our Brother
Our Father
Creator-Power that pushes forth everything into meaningfulness
Into revelation
Into making sense
Father
In the name of Jesus

Jesus
Who releases all these possibilities to us
Jesus one of us
Jesus of the flesh
Jesus the peasant
Jesus the rebel
The rebel who could shout freedom
In the teeth of the military system
That surrounded them
Their own countryside

Saying
Love your brothers
Love your enemies
Do good to those who hate you
Bless those who curse you
Feed my lambs feed my sheep
Take this bread and eat it in memory of me
Take this cup
Which is the cup of my blood of the new and everlasting covenant
The mystery of faith
Which will be shed for you and for man
For the forgiveness of sins
As often as you do it you do it in memory of me
Your sins are forgiven arise take up your bed and walk
You'll be clean of your leprosy
Why has only one returned to give me thanks

When I was hungry you fed me
When I was naked you clothed me
When I was in prison you visited me
Happy the poor in spirit for they shall inherit the earth
Happy the peacemakers for they shall be called sons of God

All these great things
Love the Lord your God
With all your heart with all your mind with all your strength
Secondly and as equal as the first
Love your neighbor your brother as yourself
And if you keep these commandments
These two
You will have obeyed the whole law

Love and be free do as you will
St. Paul said
Love
Meaning to go out to your brother
Meeting him as man
Thanking him for letting you deal with him
Serving you

It's great
It's great good news
It's great good news and it's 2000 years old
And we have been in the marketplace
Or else have been in the vineyard
Not doing our work
We have been letting the grapes rot on the vine
When we should have been picking
And feeding the world
They've been hungry for so long

No greater love has a man than this
Than he lay down his life for his friends
That's Jesus
That's our friend
Laying down his life for all of us
Standing naked before the tribunal
Before the courts of Rome
Being arrogant in a sense
Daring knowing his rightfulness

Hanged on a cross
Crying out Father forgive them for they know not what they do
Into your hands I commend my spirit
It's finished
It's completed

I love you
That's what he said
I love you men who tear up my body
Horrify my flesh
Too dumb to listen to what I have said these past years
I still love you in my dying cry
I love you I love you I love you
The good news
That's it

Peace O Father
To all men in these trying times
Peace I tell you peace peace
Peace to the peacemakers
Amen

Amen